CARING

The Soul of Leadership

Ayodeji E. Oyebola

Copyright © 2021 Ayodeji Oyeoboa

All rights reserved

The characters and events portrayed in this book are fictitious. Any similarity to real persons, living or dead, is coincidental and not intended by the author.

No part of this book may be reproduced, or stored in a retrieval system, or transmitted in any form or by any means, electronic, mechanical, photocopying, recording, or otherwise, without express written permission of the publisher.

ISBN-13: 9798585819667
ISBN-10: 1477123456

Cover design by: Loving Touch Productions
Library of Congress Control Number: 2018675309

Printed in the United States of America

Contact Information
www.emmright.com
info@emmright.com

CONTENTS

Title Page	1
Copyright	2
Dedication	5
Introduction	7
The Moment of Truth	11
Caring for Assignment	13
Caring for Vision	22
Caring for Money	31
Caring for Power	44
Caring for Knowledge	54
Caring for Self	61
Caring for Organization	74
Caring for Result	88
Caring for People	101
Final Words	112
Special Thanks	115

In loving memory of my mother, Julianah Oyebola (July 16, 1952-March 23, 2020), who taught me how to care. She excelled in her assignment as the leader of my family because she cared until the day she was called into glory.

INTRODUCTION

Leadership is one of the oldest concepts in the world but has evolved over the years. The general perception of leaders has shifted from the great man who saves the day to an emphatic individual who influences others. The personality and emotional capabilities of leaders are becoming essential for motivating followers to achieve the desired result. The followers are responding and connecting more with the leaders emotionally. One of the ways leaders can connect with the followers emotionally is to show that they care.

Caring is underrated and does not get enough recognition it deserves in leadership. Many people view caring as a mere emotional expression rather than a critical leadership action. As much as people talk about caring or like to express that they care, only a few understand its impact on leadership and organizational effectiveness. "I don't care" is one of the phrases that people use to express their frustrations. This phrase comes out when people are annoyed or feel powerless over a situation.

In organizations, the followers can often get to this point as little things can frustrate them, and they can throw their hands up in frustration. It becomes perilous when the leader gets to that point because everyone depends and draws their inspiration from the leader. The moment the leader gets to this point, it might be the beginning of the end of the team or organization. Everything goes downhill from that point, and the very essence of the establishment could be in jeopardy. Anywhere the leaders are carefree or careless, destruction awaits.

Everyone in a leadership position must lead, but everyone that leads does not have to occupy leadership positions. We do not have to hold leadership positions in institutions to lead. Some leadership roles on the job, families, religious groups, student groups, or sports teams are apparent, but many are not because they do not have formalized titles or positions.

Leadership is not a state; it is an act. Leadership is a process with specific actions rather than mere positions or titles. It is an expectation for everyone in leadership positions to fulfill the roles of a leader. However, some people in leadership positions do not act as leaders or do enough to justify their titles. On the contrary, there some individuals that do not occupy leadership roles but serve as leaders.

Caring is an act that every leader must perform. Caring is at the center of leadership because the leader must pay attention to every aspect of the organization. The leader must care for everything, including people, products, financial output, and organizational outcomes. The leader is the number one influencer in every establishment. The caring attitude of the leader is contagious; the attitude of the leader towards the establishment influences the actions of followers.

To clearly explain caring, we need to distinguish between caring and worrying. Worrying means being anxious and anticipating problems. It is easy to confuse worrying with caring. Sometimes, we believe that being nervous, panicking, or expecting something will go wrong means that we care, but caring is none of those. Caring involves showing interest, paying attention, looking out, being prepared, putting necessary measures in place, and willingness to do something if needed.

Caring is an attribute of confident leaders. Insecure leaders tend to worry, thus losing the focus of the people and vision. A leader that worries is not paying attention to achieve results but paying attention because of the fear that something will go wrong. A leader that worries will most likely micromanage people and create a complex system. Micromanagement limits creativity, thus leading to underperformance and underachievement. It also causes followers to lose their sense of responsibility and ownership.

This book focuses on how caring leads to leadership and institutional success. This book is not only for individuals in leadership positions or people aspiring to occupy leadership positions; it is for everyone. This book will add value to everyone because everyone is a leader, with or without a title. Whether you lead yourself, your family, small or large business, religious institution, sports teams, a non-profit organization, country, or any institution, this book outlines some of the areas where you should care. It also highlights how caring can help you to succeed in your leadership assignment.

THE MOMENT OF TRUTH

On a summer afternoon in 2016, an employee narrated his experience on his previous job. He said,

My former supervisor does not care for anyone or anything. He will stay in his office and will never take the time to check on us or the job. He does not care whether we are successful or not. It was tough, and I just came to work and just do what I can. If the person above me does not care, why should I?

While he was speaking, I did not pay much attention to what I heard. On my way home, I started reflecting on the question and wondered why the employee concluded that if his supervisor did not care, no one should ask him why he did not care.

The question was probably rhetorical to the employee, and he asked out of frustration, but his question made me examine the purpose of leadership and see leadership differently. I have analyzed the question several times and thought about every word. I tried to picture how the employee perceived his former supervisor. The individual was looking for inspiration from the leader, but he could not get it. All that the employee required from his leader was for the leader to care, and he will do his very best. When he perceived that the leader does not care, he concluded that he does not have to care either. He was frustrated, and he felt that it was better to let it go and seek employment elsewhere. Based on my discussion, I realized that leadership caring is the reason why followers believe and do their best to achieve the organizational goal.

I also concluded that caring is the soul of leadership. As the soul is the essence of humanity, caring is the essence of leadership. If the leader does not care, then the leader is not leading, and leadership dies at that point. The followers derive their sense of care and purpose from the leader, and they will care because the person above them cares.

Caring as an attitude is a reflection of the human mindset towards something or someone. Caring as a leadership attitude is so influential that it determines leadership effectiveness. When people sense that there is a positive attitude towards them or something, they will respond equally and do the needful.

CARING FOR ASSIGNMENT

The leadership assignment is the reason why anyone is a leader. The assignment is a summary of the purpose of leadership. Everyone in a leadership role should be able to answer the simple question, "why am I a leader?" The answer to the question determines if the leader cares, what the leader cares about, and whether the leader is even leading.

Whether the leader could answer the question clearly or not, what the leader cares about becomes apparent over time. Observant followers will be able to answer that question for many leaders. Some people are in leadership roles to do a job, some want to make money, some want to exercise power, some want to help people, some want to show career progression, and some are there for other reasons or a combination of different reasons.

Irrespective of the motive or purpose, leadership is more than a job, role, or position; it is an assignment. Leaders that care and focus on their assignment will refer to it as a calling. They see beyond the duties and tasks at hand. They are spiritually and emotionally connected to their assignments.

The simple way to understand every leadership assignment is to view it as a call to serve people and oversee resources. The size and type of leadership assignments may differ, but every leader has authority over people and resources. How the leader manages people and resources affect the destinies of the people under the influence of the leader and determines leadership effectiveness.

Leadership care sets the tone for leadership assignments. The leadership care for the assignment influences the level of commitment and effort. Leadership care also determines whether the assignment will be a success or failure.

Approaches To Leadership Assignment

Individuals view and approach their leadership assignments differently. Some leaders put the assignment ahead of themselves and work towards it. Some keep the assignment closer to themselves and takes it one day at a time. Some leaders leave the assignment behind and look at it occasionally, if at all. The position of the leadership assignment could affect the level of success, depending on the assignment and the followers.

Some leaders see their leadership assignment as a personal cross, and they bear it on their own. They are lone wolves in the jungle. They make all the decisions by themselves and view everything from their lenses. Such leaders micromanage every aspect of their organizations. Lone-wolf leaders do not see the need for a team, and if they have a team, they probably just discuss the outcome of their decisions rather than seeking ideas and suggestions. Even when others make suggestions, such leaders rarely listen or outrightly dismiss the recommendations altogether. They approach everything based on personal experiences and perspectives.

This type of approach to the assignment could work in a small and emerging organization where everything revolves around the leader. It can also work in big organizations in some instances, but such an approach diminishes the capability of the organization. There are times when leaders need to depend on their instincts to make critical decisions. After all, they are the head of the team for a reason. However, this approach can cause some team members to lose their sense of purpose and responsibility. Some might lose their passion, while some could leave the organization altogether. The approach also stifles innovation and creativity needed for competitive advantage and sustainability.

Some leaders understand that their leadership assignment is theirs, but they engage other people. Such leaders know their strengths and weaknesses, and they do not waste their time in their areas of weaknesses. The leaders engage the best hands to help in their areas of weaknesses. These leaders respect their followers and do not micromanage them but give them the freedom to do their jobs. The autonomy does not mean that the leader lacks control or understanding of what the followers are doing. The leaders still need to have a basic understanding of the tasks of the followers. The knowledge of the tasks will help the leader to ask intelligent questions, provide adequate resources, provide guidance, and see how the tasks fit into the overall goal.

Some leaders neglect their assignments altogether. They believe that the person that leads least leads the best. While there are moments when the followers need autonomy to do their jobs, it is the job of the leader to ensure that the followers have the resources necessary to do their jobs and deliver the expected results. Leaders in this category do not care for their assignments or the outcomes of the assignments. They rarely have any discussion with the followers because there is no goal or purpose.

This approach creates irresponsible followers who do not care. The followers get their sense of carelessness from the leader.

Clarity Of The Leadership Assignment

According to the Meriam Webster dictionary, an assignment is a task or piece of work given to an individual. Every assignment comes with responsibilities and expected outcomes. A significant aspect of the assignment is the expectation of results, which can sometimes describe the assignment better. The assignment of some leaders includes stabilizing organizations in crisis, redefining organizations, making organization profitable, or help an organization fulfill a specific mission. Anyone without a clear understanding of the assignment cannot deliver the expected results.

An understanding of the assignment creates a path to success. The leaders that understand their assignments will make the right decisions most of the time. They will create a good vision for the assignments, hire the best hands, allocate resources to the right tasks, and most likely get the desired outcome.

Jeffery Immelt, the CEO of GE between 2001 and 2017, said leaders have different assignments at different times. The stage of the organization, the general economic situation, and the prevailing business environment dictate the assignment of the leader. Jeffery led GE during very volatile periods, which include the early days of the dot-com era, technological bubble, economic recessions, and several geopolitical struggles. During his period, technology disrupted the industry, and his assignment was to "remake a historic and iconic company during an extremely volatile time."

Every leadership role, ranging from a family of two to a country of billions, comes with the pressure to deliver results. To achieve the desired goal, whoever occupies the leadership role must study the assignment and understand the expectations. It is crucial to understand the expected result, who expects the result, when they hope to see the result, and how they want the result.

After identifying the tasks to be performed and the expected result, the leader needs to understand the two basics of every assignment: people and resources. The leader needs to take time to identify the available resources and the co-travelers in the journey. Later in this book, there will be a discussion on why leaders need to understand the strengths of their team and how they can leverage their strengths to deliver the results.

Many leaders crumble under the pressure of expectations because they do not understand what it takes to carry out the role effectively. The clarity of the assignment comes into the picture here. The leaders must understand the purpose of their assignments and be able to put it into perspective. It is essential to understand that seeking clarity is the first task of every leader. If you do not know what you are doing or where you are going, it does not worth your time.

Imagine a building contractor that is building a home. The contractor needs to clarify the land to build on, the type of house, the budget for the project, the features of the house, special requests, expected time of completion, and many other things. The understanding will help the contractor develop an excellent architectural design and recruit the best hands for the project.

Unfortunately, many people are in leadership roles without having a good understanding of why they are in their positions. They do not know what they are supposed to do. The lack of knowledge causes many leaders to wander in the wilderness, leaving their followers disillusioned and frustrated, searching for answers and directions.

Lack of clarity fuels chaos and poor choices that can derail any assignment. Every leadership assignment comes with various opportunities and threats. When the leader does not understand the assignment, every team member will be scrambling to do whatever they think is right. There will be many options, and quite often, lack of clarity leads to poor choices. There may be short-term and accidental successes along the way, but the successes are unsustainable. Some people get fooled into thinking that small successes without direction are sufficient. Without a clear overall picture and strategy, there is no way to turn small successes into a sustainable advantage.

Accidental successes are not guaranteed because the failures that will overshadow them are just around the corner. Even when there are successes, the chaos around the organization will choke the achievements. Lack of clarity leads to frustration because followers will not know how to define or identify success. The clarity of the assignment will lead to clarified goals, well-defined success parameters, sustainable advantages, and team motivation.

Clarifying the leadership assignment helps the leader to create a clear vision, compatible mission, and perfect strategies to guide the team to achieve the desired results. A clear understanding of the assignment helps leaders combine the available resources and put people in the right positions to help deliver the desired results. Many leaders often waste resources and talents when they do not understand what they are supposed to do. They will find it challenging to allocate resources and talents to the tasks. They have a mismatch of people, tasks, and resources.

The clarity of the assignment helps leaders to position themselves as the motivator and developer of their respective teams. Leaders that do not understand their role will find it challenging to motivate and develop their followers. The followers depend on the leader for direction and inspiration. If the leader lacks the understanding of what to do, it is the blind leading the blinds; their destination is the ditch. Observant followers know when a leader lacks direction. Many followers jump the ship because they are struggling for direction or motivation.

A clear understanding of the assignment helps the leader to sort through environmental jargon and noises. Every institution has outside and inside distractions that could derail the assignment. Someone said, "a person without a strategy will be part of another person's strategy." A leader that does not understand his or her assignment will not have a strategy, and people with strategy will take advantage of the situation. The people that will disrupt the assignment could even be other members of the team. Various people within and without the organization will come to the leader with suggestions and ideas. Clarity helps the leader sort through the ideas and suggestions to identify the ones that fit the assignment.

Clarity helps leaders during difficult times. Leadership is never a smooth journey. There are moments of joy and happiness, and so are the moments of sorrow and extreme difficulties. Anyone can lead during happy times, but it takes good leaders to steady the ship during turbulent times that will surely come. The worth of a leader is known when things are not going well. It is the moment when the leader must dig deeper and bring the proverbial "rabbit out of the hat." During difficult times, everyone is looking up to the leader to do something. Every leadership assignment has bumps and bruises, but clarity builds endurance and resilience.

Clarity helps the leader to endure and remain focused on the assignment. Clarity helps the leader to stay focused and determined because the leader knows the ultimate goal. Clarity helps leaders to harness the resources and talents at their disposal to face and overcome challenges. It is easier to get out of a difficult situation when there is an adequate understanding of the bigger goal and destination. When faced with roadblocks, clarity can help the leader rethink the assignment and create a way out of the deep end.

Caring For Leadership Assignment

The leadership assignment centers on people and resources. However, the leader must creatively build a structure around people and resources to achieve the desired result. Leadership assignment involves creating and managing a vision, building a unified team, managing resources, engaging and developing people, as well as delivering results. The leader needs to be able to handle the various aspects of the assignment successfully. It is almost impossible to manage these tasks alone, no matter the size of the assignment. The leader that cares for the assignment will engage the best hands to help.

The attitude of the leader towards the assignment influences the followers. When the leader shows that he or she cares about the task at hand, the followers will do the same. The success of the assignment depends on the leader. The caring attitude towards the assignment is the best way to encourage followers to work towards the success of the assignment.

The leadership assignment is to be cherished and carefully managed. A well-nourished assignment will continue to flourish, produce the right results, and bring happiness to every team member. The success of the assignment depends on the caring attitude of the leader. The leader can be very eloquent and "talk the talk," but caring is "walk the walk."

CARING FOR VISION

The first task of any leadership assignment is the creation of the vision. The success of every leadership assignment starts with the creation of a compelling vision. The vision separates the leader from others in the team, organization, or nation. Irrespective of the type or size of the establishment, vision is not negotiable because it is the compass for the assignment. Vision is the bedrock of every organizational strategy and success. It is the foundation for the assignment and all other things. The vision brings people together and creates a path for everyone to follow.

An individual, team, organization, or nation without a vision does not have a future. A verse in the Bible says, "where there is no vision, the people perish." Imagine an organization or a country without a vision, everything will be chaotic, and everyone will be scrambling for direction, and people will do whatever seems right to them. Any organization or institution without a vision perplexes people and wastes individual talents. The chaos leads to brain drain as people seek greener pastures where there is a vision. Many teams, organizations, and nations lose talented people and struggle because they lack vision.

The leaders that do not care for the vision depend on luck. Luck is not a strategy; it is just a random chance. An organization with a leader that does not care for vision will waste valuable resources and human capital.

Leadership caring for vision requires the creation of

a clear vision and management of the vision. The creation of vision involves painting a picture of the future, while management of vision involves nurturing the vision.

Creating A Vision

According to the Dictionary, vision is the ability to think or imagine the future. For me, imagination is the keyword in the definition of vision. Vision involves seeing beyond the current situation and challenges to create something for people to believe. The people might not be able to see or imagine the vision, yet they will connect to it. The imagination of the leader is important because vision requires ambition and the desire to do something extraordinary.

Every good vision requires inspiration and creativity. Everyone can come up with a vision, but compelling visions come out of inspiration. The leader is the "spiritual head" of every team or organization, and the leader must be inspired to create a compelling vision. The inspiration that creates the vision will move the leader to share the vision and get people on board. The leader must dig deeper to analyze the past and current state of events, business environment, the sequence of events, study the innovations that have changed the status quo to develop a compelling vision. While a breakthrough idea or assignment can come in a day, visions are not necessarily created in one day because it requires fine-tunings and emotional connection with the intangibles. The leader must be able to reach his or her creative peak to bring something out of nothing. Creativity depends on imagination, and this must be in full force to create a compelling vision.

A Vision Statement With A Compelling Purpose

A vision statement is the declaration of the objectives and goals of an establishment. The vision should guide both the short and long-term activities of the organization while driving the ambition and creating a platform for success. The purpose of a vision statement is to make the vision relatable to people and create energy. Unfortunately, many vision statements lack purpose or substance. Some organizations operate the "theoretical vision" that is entirely different from the "vision-in-use." The theoretical vision is the vision statement that is written for everyone to read. The vision-in-use is the vision that the organization is actively working to achieve. The two forms of vision must correlate to create a strong vision.

Organizations with only theoretical visions have vision statements with powerful words but without purpose, inspiration, or path to accomplishment. The vision statement is created so that every member of the organization or team can read, digest, and live for the vision. The achievement of the purpose of the vision statement depends on the leader. It is not sufficient to write or present a powerful vision statement; the leader must care about the vision. Leadership care turns the theoretical vision into a vision-in-use. The vision must be the driver of the leadership actions and behaviors to influence the followers and spur them into action.

The vision must be purposeful, and the purpose must be strong enough to compel people into action. Almost everyone wants to be part of a winning team, and the vision creates the foundation for victory. Everyone wants to know why they are doing what they are doing and the intended outcome. A compelling vision touches the nerves of every member of the team. Some employees are passionate about their jobs because the organizational vision keeps them going. The vision with a compelling purpose makes the work rewarding and exciting because there is something to achieve.

A compelling vision raises self-expectations. Individuals that will typically do average works start to perform like superstars. Individuals begin to achieve more than their talents because of the purpose of the vision. Everyone will be determined to succeed and work hard to help the team. A sense of responsibility will begin to grow in the team, and team members will be encouraging one another to achieve the goal because they believe that there is something worth doing.

A compelling purpose opens the door for collaboration. Individuals that will naturally not work together or agree on anything start to work together because they believe in the vision. Everyone sees themselves as family members and sees themselves as part of something bigger than themselves. The success of the team becomes more enjoyable because everyone is pulling in the same direction. Egos are set aside for collective success because everyone sees the team's success as their successes. The chances of outside interference and betrayal become smaller because there is a bigger goal.

The leader that cares for vision ensures that the purpose of the vision is energized and sustained over time. Successful teams and organizations can become complacent. The team can take success for granted because they have always been successful. A leader that cares for vision will continue to keep the team grounded and working towards the vision.

Ambition And Optimism

A good vision is both optimistic and ambitious. A

vision is not within the immediate capability of any individual or organization. A vision is what an organization intends to do, achieve, or become in the future. Sometimes, visions can change due to environmental factors or the current state of the organization, but visions should not change consistently. For example, some companies changed their visions because of technological evolution and the internet that has changed how we live our lives. The vision of some organizations changed because of the change in the capabilities of the organizations.

It is essential to distinguish between vision and goal. These two terms are interrelated because they are both optimistic, ambitious, and futuristic. However, goals are subsets of vision. Visions have larger scopes and mostly without timelines. Goals have smaller scopes with timelines and attainable with projected capabilities. An organization can realize its vision by setting achievable goals with specific timelines.

There are three major categories of goals, which are short-term, medium-term, and long-term goals. Short-term goals are typically between one to two years. Medium-term goals are usually between three to five years, and long-term goals are usually between ten to twenty years or more, depending on the organization. For goals and visions to be purposeful, there must be a connection between the periodic goals and vision. The short-term goals must lead to medium-term goals, and medium-term goals must lead to long-term goals, and long-term goals must lead to vision.

Visions are usually unthinkable or unimaginable at the moment, especially to most people. Whatever can be achieved with the current and anticipated capability or resources is not a vision because it is not ambitious and does not stretch the imagination. The leader must see beyond the current capabilities and create a compelling vision.

The vision must be big enough to accommodate the visions and ambitions of people within the system. Every good vision generates excitement, enthusiasm, and optimism among people. A good vision should energize people to action. Some organizations have visions, but the visions are too narrow to accommodate the ambition of the organizational members. Individuals in the organization need to see themselves as part of the vision. Otherwise, they will not subscribe to the vision.

The leader also needs to create a relationship between individual visions and organizational vision. Leadership caring comes into the picture here. A vision should not only be about the ambitions of the leader or the organization alone. Individuals must see themselves as part of the vision. Every team member must wake up every morning feeling that they are contributing to something valuable and living the dream. The energy will drive everyone to work even when things are not working accordingly.

Managing The Vision

The management of the vision starts with clarifying the vision. The vision must not be abstract or ambiguous. It must be clear, concise, and understandable to everyone. Clarity of the vision makes it easy for people to plug in and work towards the vision. While the vision is expected to be big, ambitious, and stretches the imagination, people must understand and connect with it. A vision is valueless when people do not understand it. Only the creator understands an ambiguous vision, meaning that only the leader knows what he or she wants to achieve, and no one else could help achieve the vision. The leader must care enough to make people understand and connect with the vision.

A carefully developed and nourished vision attracts people. Everyone wants to be part of a viable vision. A good vision excites people and brings commitment. A leader who cares for the vision will sell the vision and get everyone to subscribe. A good leader will carry everyone along and cause everyone to own the vision. The leader must ensure that everyone has a sense of ownership of the vision.

A vital aspect of caring for the vision is selling the vision to people. Leaders must be able to persuade people to see what they see because most people are naturally skeptical of anything that stretches their imagination. Some people will see the vision as a fantasy or daydreaming. For example, when an owner of a small mom and pop shop presents a vision of reaching every home in the world, it is normal for everyone to think that the person is either insane or just too excited. The leader must make people realize that the vision is attainable and not out of reach.

Selling the vision to people involves creating an imaginary path between current events and the vision to make it practical. Creation of the short-term, medium-term, and long-term goals bridge the gap between the vision and the current events. The periodic goals break the vision down into small units and connect the current events to the proposed and imagined future.

The leader needs to realize that people will not just accept anything because the leader says so. The leader must be strategic and intentional in selling the vision to the people. Many people only believe what they can understand and rationalize with their minds. In this case, the leader has a dilemma because the vision must be beyond immediate rationalization, and the leader needs people to buy into the vision. The persuasion and marketing skills of the leader become crucial at this point. The leader needs to make people believe what she or he believes and imagines without making people look stupid or have small minds. The leader needs to understand how to reach the followers and make them believe in the vision.

The leader can get the followers to subscribe to the vision by making individuals see how the organizational vision benefits them. The followers will embrace the vision when they can connect with the vision and see themselves as parts of the vision. When people see something different, everyone will be asking about "what is in it for me?" or "how does this benefit me?" as humans naturally think selfishly. When individuals can see that the bigger picture includes their interests, they will subscribe to the vision.

The leader needs to recruit influential people within the organization to sell the vision. Influential people may or may not be managers or supervisors. Some people gain power because people love or respect them for various reasons. The influential people in the organization must be on board and fully persuaded of the vision. The influential people will sell the vision to the people under their influence.

The leader needs to live and breathe the vision. Caring for the vision requires the leader to have a personal conviction of the vision. The vision must become the lifestyle of the leader. There will be times when the vision will look like a mirage, but the leader must be self-assured, firm, unmoved, and unwavering. The leader who will lead the people to the promised land of the vision has to be able to weather the storms and remain optimistic even in the face of threats to the vision.

The leader is the custodian of the vision. The leader cannot lose sight of the vision because everyone derives their energy from him or her. The future is a product of today's vision. The leader takes care of the present and leads the team to the future by creating a vision. The leader needs to work with his or her team to create a strategic plan to achieve the periodic goals that accompany the vision.

It is not sufficient for any leader to create a vision; a responsible leader must care about the vision. The vision will not accomplish itself, and the leader will not achieve the vision individually. The leader will not do all the work required to realize the vision, but the most important job of the leader is to care for the vision. When the followers understand that the vision is important to the leader, they will care for the vision. The caring attitude of the leader towards the vision determines whether the vision is attainable or a fantasy.

CARING FOR MONEY

Several years ago, I heard the story of a group of friends that grew up together. The friends celebrated their achievements, help one another through adversity, and care genuinely about one another. After several years, they formed the group so that they can do community projects and organize activities. They appointed a leadership team and raised money to sustain the activities of the group through individual contributions and solicitation. As the financial strength of the group grew, the friends started fighting one another. There were differences of opinions on what to do with the money and the direction of the group. The friendship bond that the joy of success or pain of adversity could not destroy, money almost killed it.

It surprises me how the discussion of money rarely gets the attention of leadership experts and scholars. Most of the leadership discussions around money are usually indirect and focuses narrowly on morality. I am yet to see a leadership book with a candid and in-depth discussion about money in leadership. I believe that the debate about leadership responsibility with money is long overdue.

Most of the moral issues with leadership begin from an uncontrolled appetite for wealth and spending. There is nothing wrong with making more money or being wealthy, but the immoral acquisition of wealth and irresponsible spending is unacceptable. Immoral leaders love the fame and respect that comes with wealth. They spend uncontrollably, make risky investments, take from everyone, borrow money at every opportunity, cheat, bend the rule, take advantage of followers, and are unwilling to fulfill their obligations. Once they do not make enough money to satisfy their uncontrolled appetite, they start to "rob Peter to pay Paul." Such behaviors have led to the demise of many companies.

Some leaders have good intentions but lack the basic understanding of how money works. They fall into trouble due to financial ignorance because they do not pay enough attention to that aspect. Unfortunately, ignorance is not an excuse for bankruptcy.

Money leadership is one of the major areas where many leaders fail. It needs to gain more attention because money influences almost every aspect of human life. It is not immoral for leaders to be wealthy or express their wealth, but it is essential to emphasize how money influences leadership effectiveness.

The Power Of Money

Money is one of the pillars of society. The discussion about the power of money goes back in time. There were several discussions about money in the Bible. Two major characters in different Bible eras talked explicitly about the power of money. In the Old Testament, Solomon said, "money answers all things," and in the New Testament, Paul said, "the love of money is the root of all evils." We cannot continue to underestimate the impact of money on leadership excellence due to its effects on society. Effective leaders understand the impact of money on their organization, and they take good care of it.

Money is the most powerful commodity in the world. It has the power to make or break human lives and determine the successes or failures of organizations and nations. Money has built and destroyed many homes, businesses, organizations, and countries. We are living in a world that is under the influence of money. The 2008 financial crisis is perhaps the greatest financial crisis of all time. The crisis was due to the irresponsibility and carelessness of leaders at various levels. During the crisis, many people lost their lives, homes, jobs, businesses, and livelihoods. Many people struggled for many years to recover, while many never recovered.

Many people are in jail today because of their attitude towards money. Despite the controlling power and influence of money on our society, human beings determine the extent to which money can exert its influence. Whatever we do with money determines the results that we will get. The caring attitude of the leader towards money determines how money can dictate the success of the institutions.

The Basics Of Money

Money is a medium of exchange for products and services. Money circulates in the form of payment for goods and services. We make money when we sell goods, provide services, work, invest, or perform duties. We spend money to pay for the products and services that we receive. The net exchange of money is either a profit or a loss.

The three concepts of money are **revenue**, **expense**, and **net income**. Revenue is the money we make from the services provided, the goods sold, the wages received from the job done, the taxes collected, and others. The leader needs to know the sources of revenue and how much. Expense is the money we pay for the goods bought or services received, including wages paid, rent, cost of goods produced, utilities, and others. The leader needs to understand what is purchased and how much the items cost.

Net income is the difference between revenue and expenses. In an ideal world, every individual and organization should have a positive net income or breakeven, but that is not always the case. There are times when individuals or organizations can operate at a loss because of investments and other constructive purposes, but it should not be a norm. There must be a balance between expenses and revenue to prevent financial catastrophe. Financial responsibility begins with the understanding and application of three concepts of money.

Money Management

Money management is crucial to the sustainability of any establishment, and every leader must be proficient in it. In this context, the goal of money management is to create a balanced financial system in which the net income supports the survival of the organization. Revenue management and expense management are the two major pillars of money management. Every leader must learn to create the right balance between these two aspects.

Revenue management involves how an organization makes money. It includes the pricing of products and services, account receivable, and turnover time. The pricing analysis helps determine if the prices are appropriate compared to the cost of production. The understanding will allow the leader to determine the need for adjusting to the cost of production or selling price. Account receivable represents the money owed to an organization for goods sold or services already provided. Turnover time is the time it takes for an organization to get paid for services provided. Both account receivable and turnover time are vital for cash flow management. High account receivable and long turnover time are recipes for disaster as the organization can quickly become cash strapped. Knowledge of revenue management helps the leader to make important financial decisions.

Expense management involves how an organization spends money. It consists of the cost of producing goods and services, bill payment cycle, liabilities of the company, and cost of investments. The cost of producing goods and services includes fixed costs such as the cost of machines and building mortgage and variable costs such as wages, bills, fees, and cost of materials. The cost of investment is how much it costs the organization to make money in the future. The understanding of these expenses allows the leader to make informed decisions. Lack of knowledge of the cost of doing business could jeopardize the future of the organization.

Organizations can make future investments with the hope of making profits to offset the losses. However, it is vital to analyze the viability of investments. While there are no certainties in life, it is crucial to examine the impact of every investment on the organization. If an investment will cripple the existing business, it does not make sense to make such an investment. Some leaders make investments at the expense of the current events. It is essential to understand that the future is not guaranteed, and there is no future without the present. There needs to be the right balance between investments and current events. The leader must have a clear understanding of the short and long-term impacts of the investments on the organization's sustainability.

Financial issues arise when the organization continues to spend money without making enough money to offset the expenditures. Positive cash flow is necessary for the sustainability of any organization. The organization must be able to meet its obligation at every point in time.

The leader does not have to be an accountant or a financial expert to know whether the organization is spending more than it makes or the revenue sources and expenditure items. Every leader must know the fundamentals of the financial statements and identify the items on the reports. The key to money leadership is to know when things are not going well financially. The simple red flag is when obligations such as bills, wages, payments to vendors are coming due faster than money is coming in.

Once the leader identifies a problem or having difficulty understanding the flow of money, it is time to contact the financial experts and strategists to analyze the root cause. Financial experts are the obvious people to help with financial issues. However, the financial problems of some companies lie in their processes. Poor processes or bottlenecks affect cash flow. Organizational processes will be discussed further under Care for Organization.

The management of money is one area in which many leaders fall into deep holes. Instead of caring for the money, some leaders try to control money. They view money as a weapon or an instrument of oppression and power. Caring for money does not mean controlling the money or watching the money like a hawk. It simply means creating a system for effective making, spending, accounting, and management of money.

Some leaders prioritize money over any other thing. They view money as the only thing. While it is important to ensure that the organization is solvent and financially stable, leaders need to understand that money is only as important as the other aspects of the organization. Money is crucial to the sustainability of the organization, but it cannot be the only focus. Caring for money does not mean putting money ahead of everything or prioritizing money over personal integrity, quality of products and services, and the safety of employees and customers. Caring for money involves putting money into consideration to create a sustainable organization. In addition to that, an organization only becomes profitable when it delivers quality products and services that meet the needs of the people.

On the other hand, there are leaders with little to no understanding of how money impacts organizational success. They leave everything in the hand of the bookkeeper and continue to believe that everything will be fine. While this hands-off approach can be good at times, it is a recipe for disaster. The people in charge of the accounts could be tempted to mismanage the organizational resources or defraud the organization.

Financial Responsibility

The key to caring for money is financial responsibility. Leadership financial irresponsibility has led to many business closures, individual and family bankruptcies, and the economic collapse of many nations. Leaders are responsible for the financial health and solvency of their establishments. To prevent financial catastrophe, here are some ways that leaders can care for money.

Expense adjustments. It is good to make more money, and everyone should strive for that. However, the most reasonable way to be sustainable is to reduce expenses to match revenue until revenue improves. Some people believe that you should fake it till you make it. Having more expenses than revenue creates negative net income, resulting in financial struggles and eventual bankruptcy. The ambition to make more money is good, but every leader must know that there are times of lean and abundance. The unfortunate aspect of this is that some leaders only look to increase revenue without considering the expenses when there are financial issues.

More often than not, the problems lie in the expenses because increasing revenue is not usually easy to accomplish. For example, it is not easy to increase the price of goods and services without a valid reason. Also, it is not easy to raise new revenue without incurring more expenses. Even in profitable organizations, it is good to analyze expenses because every reduction in expenses increases profitability.

Loans are not always the solution. There are times when it is necessary to take loans, but loans should always be the last resort. It is unwise to turn to loans whenever there is a financial problem. Every loan is a liability that must be settled and mostly with interests. Some people think that loans are there for a purpose, and they must take loans. Some also believe that no one can be great unless they have debts. Some leaders have destroyed the future of their organizations by incurring debts more than the capacity of the organizations.

Whenever there is a financial deficit or need to raise money, the first thing is to see if money can be raised internally before considering loans. Organizations that can raise money internally tend to fare better because the interests on the loans become part of the bottom line. Loans can provide a reprieve, but that should always be the last resort in every circumstance.

If it is necessary to get a loan, it is vital to analyze the cost of borrowing and develop a repayment plan. Every debt comes with a cost, and the debt will be due at some time. Even interest-free loans are only for specific periods, and delayed interests will be due if the loan goes into default. Some of the consequences of defaulting on loans include future higher interest rates, loss of creditworthiness, loss of credibility, loss of collateral, bankruptcy, and many others.

In the analysis of loans and the cost of borrowing, it is vital to know the loan amount, loan period, interest rates, penalties, fees, repayment capability of the borrowing organization, among other things. Analysis of these items and other things will allow the leader to know if the organization could fulfill its current obligations and loan obligations.

While the leader may not be doing the analyses, it is good for the leader to understand all these things. The weight of the debts rests on the shoulder of the leader. The leader is responsible for the outcome of the organization. Debts reduce the current financial capacities and prospects of organizations. It can also lead to long-term problems that could impact the future of the organization.

Budgeting. Organizations need to operate on sound resource planning and allocation. A budget is a useful tool for identifying when something is off the track. It also holds everyone accountable, including the leader. Leaders that care about money understand the value of budgets. They ensure that budgets are developed and reviewed at periodic intervals to know that things are going according to plan. If necessary, budgets can be adjusted to accommodate changes in operating circumstances and the environment.

Internal control. An effective control system is non-negotiable in any organization. Unfortunately, some leaders misplace trust and control. It is essential to trust everyone that they are competent to do their jobs and do it accordingly. It is equally important to have a control system that identifies problems, whether intentional or unintentional. Many people with good intentions make mistakes, and the control system is in place to identify these mistakes and rectify them before they become more significant issues.

Most people have good intentions, but anyone can be tempted to do the wrong thing when left without control. The purpose of control is not to micromanage followers or create distrust. It is for preventing lawlessness and temptations. A system without internal control is prone to fraud.

Good leaders will not micromanage the finances, but they will put a system to ensure that everything is in order. The good practice is to build a control system into the finances and other aspects of the organization. Some leaders just wake up one day and say, I want to audit the finances. Such a decision usually implies that the leader is accusing the employees, leading to distrust. The key to avoiding such issues is to build a control system into the organizational system.

Transparency. In many families, some spouses leave everything about money to the care of one person. They do not even want to know whether bills are paid or not. While it is good to trust each other, a lack of understanding of family finances is a bad idea. I have seen a situation where the person in charge of finances in the family did not pay mortgages, leading to foreclosure. I have also seen a situation whereby a man passed away, and the wife did not know anything about the family finances or assets.

Irrespective of the type or size of any establishment, it is essential for the leaders to have discussions about money. Caring about money at every level is vital for sustainability. Every employee must know how they contribute to the finances of the organization and the effect of every dollar spent or received. If possible, every employee should have access to the budgets and financial statements of their areas at least. It promotes responsibility and accountability.

The leader that cares about money will be transparent with money. I talked to an employee of a particular organization. She respects her boss because her boss discusses the finances of the organization with every employee in the organization. She said, "Although I am not in the accounting department, he will come to all of us and say this is how much we made, and this is what we intend to do with money." Based on the understanding, she knows the financial status of the organization and how she contributes.

Caring For Money

A leader can either lead money or be led by money. The attitude of the leader towards money determines whether the leader will lead money or be led by money.

The leaders that are led by money do not care about money. There are two types of leaders in this category. The first sets of leaders that are led by money will do anything to get money. They usually understand the concept of money and money management, but the influence that money has on them causes them to mismanage money. They have uncontrolled appetites for money. The other sets of leaders that are led by money have little to no knowledge about money. Their ignorance about money causes them to fall at the feet of money.

The leaders that lead money care for money. They see it as a tool and treat it as such. They understand the concept of money management and use money as a tool to achieve their goals. They are financially responsible and consider the sustainability of the organization when making financial decisions.

Good leaders understand the impact of money on the sustainability of their organizations, and they know that their attitude to money sets the tone for the followers. Good leaders are morally sound and hold themselves accountable like any other member of the organization. They consider how the organization makes and spends money.

Unethical leaders open the door for the followers to justify inappropriate behaviors. Ethical leaders that care for money are not greedy and will not take advantage of customers or vendors. They ensure that the organization honors its financial commitments to everyone within and outside the organization. Their organizations are financially sound and follow all financial laws and regulations. They ensure that the organization is not burdened with debts but remain financially solvent.

Sometimes, leaders struggle between money and quality. It is essential to care for the customers because businesses do not exist without them. Organizations cannot fulfill their promises to their customers without money, and employees will not work for free. It is imperative to strike a balance between money and quality of products and services. Compromise on quality is never the right way to create balance, and raising prices should not always be the first option. Cost and process analysis will determine the best course to proceed with pricing.

Whether a family leader or the CEO of a multinational corporation, a basic understanding of money is non-negotiable. Many promising families and businesses have fallen apart because of money. It is not all the leaders of bankrupted companies that were irresponsible. Some were due to the lack of basic knowledge of money or lack of attention towards money. Some people go into debt because of cash flow. On paper, they make enough money, but the cash is coming slower than liabilities. Process evaluation and financial analysis might be necessary. Happy spenders must learn to reduce expenses and spend within their means. Every leader that cares about money must create a healthy balance between revenue and expenses.

CARING FOR POWER

Power separates leaders from followers. Leadership is a function of power, and power is a function of influence. Leaders use power to influence people to lead them in a particular direction or achieve specific goals. Leadership is not a function of position but a function of influence and power. While leadership positions automatically come with power, some people are powerful and influential yet without occupying any leadership positions.

Most leaders do not realize the extent of the influence of their powers. Leadership power does not only affect the lives of followers; it indirectly affects the lives of people that are related to their followers. Followers of leaders who use powers positively will be happy, which could positively impact the families and friends of the followers. On the other hand, followers of leaders who use the power to intimidate will struggle, negatively affecting their personal lives. For instance, how a supervisor exerts power on the subordinates at work affects how the subordinates relate with their families and friends. Some people commit suicide or lose their families because of their leaders.

Leadership power has long-lasting effects beyond the current areas of influence. In one way or the other, every leader model their leadership philosophy after someone. Some leaders model their leadership philosophies based on their first leader. If their leadership model abused power, they would probably emerge as an abusive leader.

Forms Of Power

Social psychologists John French and Bertram Raven identified the five forms of power as coercive, legitimate, reward, referent, and expert powers. These powers are apparent in the way in which individuals carry themselves and relate with people.

Coercive power is the use of force by a leader to make followers perform a specific task. Threats of punishment usually follow the use of force if the followers do not comply. Leaders that adopt coercive power create fear in people so that they could achieve their goals. This type of power is easily misused and creates psychological stress for followers. Leaders that depend on coercive power create toxic environments that could lead to discomfort and dissatisfaction. Coercive power is unsustainable because once the fear factor is lost, the power becomes useless. Coercive power is not a reliable form of power but can be useful in situations where change is inevitable, but people are unwilling to embrace change.

Legitimate power, otherwise known as positional power, is the power that is associated with the position that an individual occupies. This is the power that comes as a default for everyone in a leadership role. Leaders that rely on this type of power believe that followers should fear, obey, or respect them based on their positions. Legitimate power could be used in conjunction with reward and coercive power. Individuals that depend solely on legitimate power use their position to intimidate followers to get things done. They can also use their position to influence rewards or compensation. Legitimate power increases as individuals move up in the organization. However, the power becomes irrelevant when the individual is no longer occupying the role that gives them power.

Reward power refers to the use of incentives by the leader to influence the followers to perform specific actions. The followers that comply will be rewarded, while those that do not comply will not get the reward. The reward power is based on the exchange of something valuable for action. The rewards could range from tangibles such as money to intangibles such as praise or appreciation. The leaders that depend on the reward power believe that people will do things when rewards are in place. The primary issue with reward power is that the reward must correspond with the action. If the reward does not correspond, the desired action may not be performed.

Referent power is a power based on influence generated from people. This type of power is usually based on the personality of the leader. Individuals with referent powers do not gain power due to position or reward. Referent power is gained from approval, acceptance, or admiration from people. Individuals with referent power may or may not occupy leadership positions, but they get power because they influence their environment. Charismatic leaders usually use referent power because people are attracted to them. The followers work very hard and look for the approval of leaders with referent because they admire the leader. The primary issue with referent power is that it can be abused, and people can be misled.

Expert power is based on knowledge, expertise, skills, know-how, and intelligence. An individual with expert power gain followers based on their ability to solve problems or provide useful information that adds value. Leaders with expert power can persuade people to do something because the followers trust their judgments. The followers respect the opinions of a leader with expert power because they believe that the leader makes intelligent decisions, and every action is based on a good understanding of situations. Expert power can diminish as the followers continue to gain more knowledge and insight.

Depending on the capability of the leader, more than one of the forms of power can be available to the leader, which can be used at different times. Individuals with expert and referent power tend to excel more than others because people respect them for knowledge and admire them for their personalities. Leaders must analyze situations to know the type of power to adopt.

Attitude Towards Power

The general view of an individual about life significantly influences attitude towards power. Our perspectives shape how we treat others. Individuals with pessimistic views of other people will use their power to dominate and oppress others, while individuals with optimistic views will use their power to build others.

Individuals with pessimistic views are generally less trusting and believe that the world is dangerous. They see the world as survival of the fittest, and only the strong ones will survive. They think that you should only trust yourself, and everyone does everything mainly for selfish interests. This school of thought believes that if you have power, you must use it as much as you can. The leaders with this perspective tend to be more autocratic and develop systems that emphasize laws, control, and discipline. Such leaders hold power dearly and use it as much as they can. They can also use power to manipulate others as long as it furthers their interests.

Individuals with optimistic views of people believe in the goodness of humanity. They see the good in people and think that we can all coexist. The people with this view of life tend to be open and trusting. Optimistic leaders create open environments that engender trust and interpersonal relationships. They see themselves as part of the team rather than the head of the team. They use their power to develop people and make them feel comfortable.

Douglas McGregor's Theory X and Theory Y gave us a clear indication of how our view of others can predict our attitude towards power.

The leaders that adopt Theory X have pessimistic views of human beings. Theory X leaders believe that people are lazy and will avoid work if they can. Based on that, employees must be closely supervised and monitored. They establish a rigid and strict control system with a clearly defined hierarchy. Theory X leaders believe that people will not work without incentives or threats of punishment.

The leaders that adopt Theory Y have optimistic views of people. Such leaders believe when people are in the right environment, they can be responsible, hardworking, ambitious, and productive. Theory Y leaders do not believe in threatening people or provide specific incentives to achieve organizational goals. Instead of threats or incentives, they encourage followers to develop internal motivation by creating an enabling environment for individual development. Theory Y leaders do not minimize incentives or financial rewards; they do not make it the primary means of motivation.

It is worth noting that Theory X and Theory Y models are the two extremes of leadership perspectives. Most leaders fall somewhere in between the two extremes.

Some are closer to Theory X, and some are closer to Theory Y. It is not uncommon for some leaders to be careful and try to understand situations and people. There are good and bad people, and being cautious is not out of place. However, cautiousness and pessimism are not the same because of their approach to people and power.

Theory Y leaders believe that people are innocent until proven guilty, while Theory X leaders believe that people are guilty until proven innocent. Careful leaders believe in people and allow people to display their talents while putting control systems in place to prevent and identify issues.

Fear Or Respect

The perspectives of leaders on power determine whether followers will fear or respect them. The leaders who adopt the fear factor will use their power to intimidate people and create an intimidating culture. Some leaders believe that the fear that they create in their followers helps them to achieve the desired result.

The leaders that use the fear factor use legitimate, coercive, and reward power mostly. They want to be the face of everything and are keen to emphasize their positions, powers, and influence. They flaunt their achievements and use power to determine the destinies of people. They demand respect and are eager to point out how they are better than others. Such leaders create and emphasize the power distance between themselves and their followers. They do not take criticism, unaccountable to anyone, and care so much about their interests.

Such leaders see inequality as an advantage. They consider inequality as a way of establishing superiority and dominion. They emphasize that life is not fair, and everyone should accept it and live with it. Life is not fair, but leaders must reduce inequalities as much as possible.

The leaders who lead by fear always emphasize their positions and make it clear that they hold the key to everything. They hold on to power and will not allow anyone to share their power. They see themselves as all in all and ensure no one can do anything without them. They consistently display their power, treat the followers like subjects, and see people as disposables.

Most autocratic leaders rule with fear because they are afraid and insecure. They rule with iron hands and micromanage every aspect of the system. They do not mind undermining their followers as long as it fulfills their interest. They rarely develop leaders because the rise of other people threatens them. They are transactional and base everything on rewards and punishment. The people that align with them get rewarded, while the people that antagonizes them get punished. They try to punish all offenses because forgiveness opens the door for more offenses. Such leaders are careful not to allow anything to diminish their powers and fear factor.

Leaders that lead by fear stunt the growth of their followers and cause emotional damage. Such leaders do not want their followers to grow. The fear factors cause the followers to be afraid of making mistakes, speak their minds, or share ideas. Such leaders are quick to suppress ideas and creativity because they do not want anyone to be better than them.

On the other hand, the leaders who gain the respect of their followers tend to downplay their legitimate, coercive, and reward powers. They use their referent and expert power to develop others. They focus on working with people and are humble enough to accept their mistakes.

They eliminate the power distance and enjoy working with their followers. They develop positive professional and personal relationships with their followers and build trust within the team. They look for the good in the people and use their power to build people. Their followers and other people outside their circle of influence respect them.

The respected leaders who care about power measure success by the number of people they help. They consider the success of their subordinates as an integral part of the success of their assignment. While they do not lose sight of the big goal, they help their followers achieve personal goals and self-actualization.

Good leaders are usually emotionally intelligent. They consider the physical and emotional well-being of their followers. Therefore, they are aware of how their powers could cause emotional damage to their followers. The leaders that gain the respect of their followers are open. They encourage their followers to work freely with them. They are always willing to help and do not consider themselves to be too important to do anything.

Leaders that care about power create an environment that is free of fear and oppression. They believe that fear has torment and adds no value to them or their followers. They want their followers to be more successful than them. Such leaders provide their followers with opportunities and challenges for growth.

Respect can only be earned but not demanded. Followers will not respect the leader because the leader demands respect. The leaders that rule by fear demand respect, while the leaders that remove fear automatically gain respect. Respect is reciprocal and earned when the leader respects the followers and makes them feel like human beings. Leaders are respected based on their actions and the use of power.

The use of power by the leaders determine whether the leader will be feared or respected. The leaders that rule by fear becomes irrelevant once the followers are no longer under their influence. On the other hand, followers usually maintain positive relationships with a respected leader, even when they are no longer under the influence of the leader.

Fear damage relationships, but respect builds relationships. The respect and fear in leader-follower relationships have their roots in the leadership use of power. Leaders that care about power focus on building relationships with their followers. They create a positive environment that eliminates fear but fosters teamwork and respect.

Caring For Power

Leadership power is both constructive and destructive. The attitude of the leader towards power determines whether the result will be the former or the latter. Leaders can build or ruin lives and families by their powers. Leaders need to understand how their subordinates view their use of power because it is crucial to the success of their assignments. The leaders that care about power understand the impact of their power on followers. They do everything possible to ensure that they are not using their power to intimidate or oppress people.

The leaders that care for power know when to use the appropriate type of power. Every leader will not get it right every time, but a pessimistic view of people can lead to misuse of power. Optimistic people are not opposed to laws and control but use them to promote good practices rather than creating fear. Rules and controls are supposed to serve as guides rather than instruments of oppression.

Leaders do not need to display the strength of their powers all the time. The measure of the strength of a leader does not lie in the display of power. It lies in compassion and quality of judgment. Based on the position, the followers are already under the influence and control of the leader. How leaders express their powers determines whether the follower will fear or respect the leader.

CARING FOR KNOWLEDGE

Vision is the picture of the future, but knowledge creates the future. Knowledge is power. The knowledge power of organizations determines the success of the organization in the current economy. The explosion of the internet of things has made a lasting change in the way we live our lives. Internet-based technologies have become integral parts of our lives. The world has become smaller, and everyone has the world at their fingertip. We conduct personal and professional businesses with people around the globe through the internet. Geographical locations and distances are no longer a barrier. Individuals, teams, businesses, and nations around the world are vying for a competitive advantage over one another.

The old-fashioned way of holding on to an idea and profiting from it is over. Individuals and organizations must keep evolving in the current economic landscape. The key to continuous evolution is knowledge, and the knowledge also must develop and reproduce speedily to cope with the market demands. Knowledge in this context refers to the ideas, information, and expertise. The leader must care about the organizational knowledge-base because any organization without a sound and evolving knowledge base cannot compete in the global economy.

The ideas that will take organizations to the next

level lie in the organization. The leader must manage, maximize, care for organizational knowledge. Although knowledge could be gained from other sources, the knowledge and ideas of the current members of the organization fit directly into the system because the people understand the system. Knowledge and ideas that are shaped within the organization are readily applicable to solve organizational problems.

Knowledge Management And Knowledge Sharing

Organizational knowledge is an intangible asset of the organization. Balance sheets are usually used to measure the value of organizations because the balance sheets have tangible data that can be measured. However, the real value of any organization is its knowledgebase. Organizational ideas, expertise, and information create the data on the current and future balance sheets. Top organizations such as Amazon, Facebook, Google, Apple, Tesla, and Microsoft with giant balance sheets have strong knowledge bases.

The development of the organizational knowledge base involves knowledge management, which is the effective handling, arrangement, creation, sharing, and distribution of knowledge within the organization. The leaders that care about knowledge are knowledge managers. They find ways to combine individual knowledge to develop the organizational knowledge base.

Knowledge management could sound like an expensive project for smaller organizations, but it can be done with little to no resources. The leader needs to be intentional by creating an open environment that allows the followers to express their thoughts and ideas. The leader can also provide opportunities for individuals and teams to document and present their knowledge and ideas.

Knowledge can only be managed when shared, and leaders must encourage their followers to share knowledge. Knowledge sharing is at the center of knowledge management because it involves exchanging ideas, expertise, experience, information, and thoughts among organizational members to create new knowledge or solve problems. Knowledge sharing occurs unintentionally in most places, but the environment can determine whether the followers will continue to share knowledge. Caring leaders ensure that knowledge sharing occurs continually to develop new knowledge and ideas.

Knowledge is power, but knowledge sharing creates a superpower. When ideas are combined, it removes the weaknesses of individual ideas and combines the strengths of the ideas. The combined ideas will be refined and useful for addressing organizational issues.

Benefits Of Knowledge Management

Knowledge management provides organizations with significant benefits ranging from simple problem-solving to competitive advantage in the global marketplace. Some of the benefits include:

Improved problem-solving. Organizations face challenges in varying degrees from time to time. Problems can be effectively solved when organizational members can come together to discuss the issues. Each member has different backgrounds, experiences, and expertise. The combination of these experiences and expertise can help in solving organizational problems. There are times when organizations need external consultants to help, but many problems can be solved internally because the members have a better understanding of the system and its functions.

Internal solutions to organizational problems are cost-effective and adaptable because the problem solvers have a better knowledge of the organization. Knowledge sharing could also help teams and organizations deal with external threats. Continuous collaboration among the members provides the constant flow of information to combat threats of competitors and adversaries. Individuals get information from various sources, and information from one person could be beneficial. When everyone can express their ideas and share information safely, the impact of internal and external threats can be mitigated.

Ideas and innovation. The difference between successful and struggling organizations sometimes lies in their ability to develop new ideas. Individual knowledge and experience give birth to ideas, creativity, and innovation. In an environment where individuals can express themselves, there will be a flow of ideas because of the freedom to experiment and express ideas. These ideas can contribute to the development of new products and services that could lead to financial returns and competitive advantage. The ideas of some individuals have propelled many organizations to the top of their industries.

Development of a learning organization. Organizations that encourage knowledge sharing have tendencies to become learning organizations. Peter Senge identified a learning organization as an organization that facilitates the learning of its members and change continuously. Taking the term literally, a learning organization is the one that promotes learning among its members. Team learning is one of the main pillars of a learning organization. Team learning involves open discussion and sharing of knowledge to facilitate learning and solve problems.

Learning organizations are efficient and effective. They also have higher levels of innovation and a better understanding of customer needs, leading to profitability and competitive advantage. The employees are also satisfied due to mental freedom, which enhances personal growth and development.

Cost-effective training system. Organizational members gain more skills as they share knowledge continuously. Individual developments through knowledge-sharing lead to improved performance and productivity. In the current labor market, turnover is an expectation as employees always search for greener pastures. Organizations will lose significant knowledge when an employee moves on. Knowledge sharing will help to cushion the loss of the employee by retaining the knowledge within the organization.

Caring For Knowledge

Vision is the map of a future destination, but knowledge is the vehicle that takes you to that destination. Anyone can dream of a beautiful future, but a lack of knowledge will either leave you in your current state or take you to the wrong destination. Any visionary leader must care about knowledge.

The benefits of knowledge in the 21st century make it inevitable for leaders to care for knowledge. As stated earlier, knowledge sharing is the most crucial aspect of knowledge management, and knowledge sharing occurs more in informal settings. While many work environments cannot be entirely casual, leaders need to create environments that are conducive for sharing knowledge.

The leaders that care for knowledge create knowledge environments. Such environments are relaxed and conducive for self-expression and open discussions. In an open environment, there is trust and interpersonal relationships. The people are free to express themselves and share knowledge without fear of stolen ideas or repercussions. The open environment is the breeding ground for ideas, knowledge sharing, creativity, and innovation.

The behaviors of the leader influence the organizational culture. The team environment is a picture of the team culture. How leaders conduct themselves influences how the team will react, thus making the leadership behaviors more critical in developing knowledge environments.

Happiness and psychological safety enhance creativity. Happy teams work together and help one another. In one of my research works, I found that honesty and openness are two of the most crucial leadership behaviors that influence the desire to share knowledge.

Leadership honesty improves leadership trust and security among followers. An honest leader will not show favoritism, take credit for other people's work, or backstab others. Instead, the leader will provide timely feedback, hold everyone accountable, give due credits, invest in the growth of the followers, and care for individuals and teams. Honesty creates the psychological safety required for sharing ideas. When followers feel safe, they tend to be more expressive and willing to help one another.

An open leader is willing to receive feedback, humble enough to learn from the followers, accept personal mistakes, take responsibilities, tolerate honest mistakes, and encourage followers to express themselves. There are times when mistakes give birth to new ideas. The history of Post-it notes at 3M is a typical example of how mistakes can lead to ideas. The person that discovered post-it notes was trying to do something else but could not get the desired result. Many people are buying the "mistake" that was made many years ago. It takes an open leader to allow the mistake to grow into a valuable product. The opportunity to share mistakes can also be a lesson for others if the environment allows it.

Openness increases interpersonal relationships, which are essential for knowledge sharing. Individuals tend to share knowledge with a person that they are comfortable with. In a closed environment, knowledge sharing will decrease because followers will not be willing to engage one another. Everyone will be cautious and focused on their jobs.

The leader sets the tone for the environment. The leader who cares about the knowledge base of the team must ensure that the environment is conducive for knowledge sharing. The future of the organization depends on the knowledge of the team. The leader that cares must ensure that knowledge is shared continually within the team. The leader must ensure that the environment supports knowledge sharing and individual members see value in making their knowledge available to the team. The leader must also lead by example in sharing knowledge.

CARING FOR SELF

In many instances, people view leaders as strong, powerful, emotionless, and unmovable. However, the leader is not a superhero but a human, just like any other person. The leader also needs care. If a leader does not care for him or herself, why should others care? The leaders are different from other people in positions or roles and responsibilities but not in composition.

The leader, like any other person, has a spirit, soul, and body. The leader has emotions and can lose temper, cry, laugh, make mistakes, and do what other people do. The leader also has a human body that can get tired. Some followers see their leaders and a superhuman and sometimes forget that leaders go through what everybody on earth goes through.

I was talking to a friend some time ago. She told me that her supervisor seems moody and unfriendly that day. I asked whether that is the supervisor's usual demeanor, she said no. She told me that her supervisor is one of the best people she has ever met. She stated that her supervisor is always very understanding, friendly, and always willing to help. I advised her to check on her supervisor and ask if she could help in any way.

Many times, people forget that the leaders go through what everyone goes through. The leaders have personal lives that can influence their actions and behaviors. The leaders are not immune from life struggles and do not have an extra life. They are vulnerable to life circumstances. However, I am not blaming the people for seeing the leaders as superheroes. Many leaders portray themselves as superheroes and heavenly beings that do not go through life or need help.

It is essential to recognize that leaders are human beings, and their whole beings need care. Everyone, including the leaders themselves, needs to remember that leaders are not robots but humans with feelings and emotions. Some leaders also tend to forget themselves when dealing with everyone and everything.

The leaders need to learn to take care of themselves to have the strength to take care of other things. There is an analogy that I usually use when I talk to people about self-care. After boarding the plane, all airlines typically go through the safety instructions. There is a point when they instruct all passengers to wear oxygen masks if oxygen drops. They strictly advise everyone to wear their oxygen masks first before helping anyone, including kids. The reason is that once you cannot breathe anymore, you cannot help anyone. This analogy is also applicable to leaders. Once you lose your health, well-being, integrity, freedom, and everything that makes you who you are, you cannot help your family, team, organization, or country.

There are two significant aspects of the life of the leader that needs care: The inner self has to do with taking care of the spirit, soul, and body. The other aspect is the outer self, which is how others perceive the leader. These two aspects are intertwined and influence each other continuously. It is imperative to care for these two aspects simultaneously.

Inner Self Care

The inner self-care involves caring for our physical,

mental, and spiritual selves. Everybody has the human trinity, which includes the spirit, soul, and body. This trinity is the core aspect of the inner self, which directly influences the outer self. We only display what is inside us. The human trinity influences our perspectives, thoughts, behaviors, reactions, and life in general. Leaders need to understand themselves and take care of their whole selves.

The first step to taking care of oneself starts with the knowledge of oneself. Self-discovery is one of the aspects of life where many people fail. I have seen so many people follow the crowd and do what others do. They follow the trends without understanding whether what they are doing conforms to their body systems. When I was in college, many students used to read at night because it is quieter. However, some of these students sleep in class because they were awake all through the night. As a result, many of them performed poorly. I tried to read overnight too, but I stopped it after two days because I understood my system. I love to read with distractions. My mind wanders when everything is quiet, which means I cannot concentrate.

Every leader needs to take time to know who they are and how they react to situations. The leaders need to understand their body system to know when they hit the red zone and need to recharge. The body is the central figure of who we are, and without proper care for the body system, we will lose ourselves. We need to know the peak period of our bodies and how stress affects our body systems. We need to understand our sleep system and how it affects our bodies.

The second part is to understand how our mind operates. In the example above, I talked about how I love to read with background noise because my mind wanders when everything is quiet. While it is difficult for me to read without noise, I love to have quiet moments because my mind only functions when I have the time to think. I get the opportunity to analyze situations and think about all the hows, whats, whens, and whys. I find my strength in the sharpness of my mind, and without my thinking moment, I cannot operate at my peak. Some people operate differently. They cannot read without absolute silence because every pin drop distracts them. Some people enjoy the chaos because they create patterns in chaos and make the best of it. Some people are so gifted that their minds will operate in any circumstance.

The third part of the human trinity is the spirit. As much as we try to disconnect ourselves from the spiritual world, we are all spiritual beings. Spirit controls the soul and body. Our spirits connect us to something greater than us, and we need to nourish our spiritual selves. A negative spirit disrupts the mind and weakens the body, while a positive spirit energizes the mind and strengthens the body. One of the things that I do daily is to pray and read my Bible. It helps me to connect to something bigger than myself and set the tone for my day. My favorite books of the Bible are Proverbs and Ecclesiastes. These two books of the Bible teach me daily living and human relationships. I take time to nourish my spiritual self so that I can be in good shape and be ready for the challenges of the day.

Some people confuse spirituality with religion. While there are some connections between the two, it is essential to stress every religious person does not have spiritual connections or gets spiritual rejuvenation from religious activities. Some people are so focused on religion that they forget the God that they are serving. Some people serve the religious leaders and have connections with the individuals and the building than God.

I understand that some people have different views on the existence of God, and my aim is not to get into that argument. My purpose is to encourage everyone, especially leaders, to work on discovering their spiritual beings. We need to know who we are spiritually and how it influences our whole being. Irrespective of personal beliefs, leaders need to understand and care for their spiritual beings to function effectively in their roles.

We live in a fast-changing environment where the roles of the leaders are changing as they react to the changing business climate. Self-discovery allows the leaders to know who they are and how the environment influences them. It will also help leaders to create a personal strategic plan on how to deal with environmental changes.

Self-discovery helps us to understand how we feel, act, and perceive that world. We can understand ourselves by taking self-assessment tests. Some of these tests help us to know when we are at our bests and worsts. They also help us understand who we are, and some of them give us suggestions on what we need to do.

Apart from the self-assessment tests, I will encourage everyone to embark on a personal self-discovery journey. The journey includes reflections on our victories and defeats, best and worst moments, as well as successes and failures. We need to reflect on the things that worked and those that did not work in those moments. We also need to study our systems as we perform our daily activities. We need to look at how our body reacts to our daily activities. These activities will help us develop a better understanding of ourselves to take care of ourselves and lead productive lives. We can only care, manage, or change what we know.

After discovering ourselves, the second step of our inner self-care is self-acceptance. Until we accept ourselves, we will only be trying to be who we are not. It is vain to run the race of others. Self-acceptance gives us the freedom to improve ourselves rather than trying to be someone else. The inner freedom from self-acceptance allows us to focus on our strengths rather than our weaknesses. We will be able to maximize our strengths and partner with others to help our weaknesses. Self-acceptance also helps us to manage our bodies, minds, and spirit better. If we are conflicted or refuse to accept ourselves, it is difficult to care for or improve ourselves.

The third step of the inner self-care is doing something about what we discover about ourselves. The only person that can help others is a person that is in the right condition. As leaders, it is vital to manage our bodies, minds, and spirits to function optimally.

We can take good care of our bodies through proper nutrition, exercise, and rest. Food is essential for nutrients, growth, energy, strength, repair of the body, and a healthy immune system. The type of food that we eat and the timing can affect the proper functioning of our body system. We need to eat good food and a balanced diet at the right time. We also need physical exercise to keep our bodies in the right shape and function properly. Physical exercises relieve stress and improve cognitive functioning.

Our sleeping habits significantly affect our body system. Someone said the best time to get things done is between 3:00 am and 7:00 am. While that is true for some, it is unproductive for many. I am one person that values my night sleep, and if I do not get enough rest, it will negatively affect my day. The most important thing is to understand how our bodies react to situations. Some people sleep early while some sleep late. Irrespective of the time that we sleep, we must ensure that we get enough sleep for the proper functioning of our bodies.

Adequate sleep, physical exercise, and a balanced diet enhance productivity and effectiveness. The human body and mind are connected. When the body is not in the right shape, the mind will struggle to perform. The body is the frame and the physical house of the soul and spirit. An effective body system is essential for the proper functioning of every human being.

The human mind is a battleground, and our minds influence how we act. As the saying goes, "if you cannot win the war within, you cannot win the war without." We need to develop our minds to face the challenges of life. We can take care of our minds through activities such as reading, reflection, and meditation. Leaders need to have a better understanding of issues concerning themselves, their followers, and their environment.

Reading books on various topics will help leaders to gain knowledge and have broader perspectives. Leaders that read will likely make better and informed decisions because of the knowledge they gain. Reflection allows us to revisit our daily activities and lessons learned from various sources. We can develop our minds and improve our responses to future events through lessons from past experiences. Meditation helps us to clear our minds, grow emotionally, and enhance our focuses. When we meditate on certain things with an open mind, we will have clarity about the situation. Meditation can reduce emotional reactions to issues and improve mental health. Working with coaches and mentors can also help to manage stress and improve capabilities.

As stated earlier, we are spiritual beings. We need to

develop our spirits, like our souls and bodies. Engaging in spiritual activities such as singing, praying, reading, and meditation will help us connect with a higher power. Our connection to the higher power will help us to develop our spirits. We can get a broader perspective and purpose of life when connected to the spiritual world. Understanding the spiritual realm and our spiritual selves can help us accept some realities and focus on the right things.

The inner self-care provides the foundation for the outer self. Physical, spiritual, psychological, and emotional cares are essential for leaders. The inner self-care enhances emotional intelligence, sanity, knowledge, internal freedom, good health, and better decision-making that are essential for good leadership.

Outer Self Care

Outer self-care involves the image and perception of the leader. The leader is at the center of everything, and how people perceive the leader influences organizational success. As many scholars have stated, organizational culture is a reflection of leadership behaviors. Followers and other people pay attention to the leader and observes how the leader carries him or herself. Outer self-care requires paying attention to personal values, behaviors, knowledge, and reaction of others.

Our values dictate our priorities. We naturally care for the things that align with our values and oppose the things that do not. Our values influence our behaviors because we live by our values. Our values motivate us, guide our decisions, and affect our relationships. Leaders need to identify their values and understand how their values affect how others perceive them.

The values of the leaders become the values of the

team. To identify our values, we must be open-minded and avoid self-deception. There are times that we do not want to accept that we value some things because of the negative public perception of those things. Any value that we are not proud to have, we probably need to change it.

After identifying our values, we need to know the hierarchy of those values. How do our values rank, and which ones can we forgo when we have to choose? For example, if a person values friendship, winning, and freedom. These are good values, but if someone values winning more than the other two, it means that the person will do whatever it takes to win. In this case, winning could trump friendship and freedom. On the other hand, if someone values friendship more than the other two, the person can give up on winning and personal freedom to keep their friends.

One of the most excellent human values is integrity. Can people trust whatever we say and accept that it is true? The moment a leader loses integrity, it is the beginning of the end. Followers will care less about the mission of the organization, and productivity will suffer. The followers will start to doubt the motive and credibility of the leader.

Integrity relates to honesty, as honesty relates to trust. Honesty is the pillar of integrity and the hallmark of a good leader. A leader that cares for integrity will not lie to get out of difficult situations. Everyone wants to claim that they have integrity, but can we boldly say that our integrity trumps any other value? Any perception of lack of integrity strips the leader of credibility, respect, and honor.

Our behavior is the product of our values. Behavior is how we act or conduct ourselves toward others. Whatever we value determines how we treat others, and the hierarchy of our values can make our behaviors inconsistent at times. When things are going well, almost everyone will do what is right. The real test of our values comes when faced with challenges. During this time, our value priority takes over the way we act.

Leadership behaviors or characters reflect the values of the leader and create the perception of the leader in the mind of others. While we have all heard that perception is not usually the reality, perception creates realities for others when it comes to leadership. The leaders need to know how their followers and others perceive them within and outside the organization. Once people perceive the characters of the leader to be questionable, every other thing becomes problematic from that point.

Leaders of questionable character do things that threaten the well-being of others, such as showing favoritism, lying, cutting corners, and demeaning others. Good leaders are perceived to be respectful, compassionate, fair, open-minded, honest, selfless, and helpful. Some leaders are deceptive and know how to manipulate people to think that they have good intentions when they have bad intentions. Bad leaders can only deceive people for some time because deception does not last forever. Over time, people will start to realize the motives of the leader. For leaders, damaged reputations are difficult to repair because broken trust leads to questionable motives.

Developing good characters starts with self-reflection and self-acceptance. Outer self-care intersects with the inner self-care in this area. Every leader must evaluate his or her behaviors and values to treat others well and create good perceptions. We can develop good characters by reading and learning from other good leaders. We need to be open, honest, and willing to change in our quest for character development. Some people read books to justify their behaviors rather than see growth opportunities. They focus on the aspects of the books that resonate with them while discarding anything that contradicts their views.

Knowledge is another area that affects the image of the leader. Leaders need to be knowledgeable about their assignments and other aspects of life. Leaders cannot know everything, but it is good for the leader to have a general view of how things operate within their team. Followers respect knowledgeable leaders. The followers of knowledgeable leaders are confident because they see their leader as a resource.

As they say, if you think knowledge is expensive, try ignorance. An unknowledgeable leader is a disservice to their team or organization. The followers look up to the leader for answers in challenging moments. The reputation of the leader takes a hit when the leader is not knowledgeable enough to help in difficult moments. The leader needs to devout resources and time to gain knowledge.

Leaders can gain knowledge by studying their assignments, reading books and articles, attending seminars and conferences, connecting with other leaders, and participating in communities of learning. The leader must be hungry for knowledge and promote learning among followers. A knowledgeable leader will improve the followers and add value to the organization as a whole.

The outer self-care creates the foundation for the success of the leadership assignment. Leaders are the focal point of every organization. Every leader must care about how people interpret their actions and behaviors. The image and behaviors of the leader influence the actions of the followers and affect the organization. Leadership perception is directly proportional to leadership success. Every leader needs to develop and enhance their reputations to lead successfully.

Caring For Self

Self-management is an integral part of emotional intelligence. Our emotional state is directly related to our well-being and perception. The way we manage ourselves determines how we work with others. Our perceptions by others influence our relationships and respect by others.

Every leader must have a philosophy. A leadership philosophy is a set of personal beliefs and principles that guides how the leader evaluates information and responds to situations. Developing a leadership philosophy is an essential aspect of self-care because it regulates our behaviors.

A clarified leadership philosophy helps the leader to remain consistent in varying circumstances. Clear leadership philosophies create consistency and fairness in the organization. The followers know what to expect all the time. They can confidently approach situations in the absence of the leader because they know what the leader will do.

As part of self-care, leaders need to mindful of their relationship with their followers. Leaders should not be committing atrocities or colluding with their followers to do evil. It affects the reputation of the leader and puts the leader in a corner. It is difficult for any leader to address the things that followers know that they do.

Leaders should endeavor to set time apart for vacation and time off. The organization must have a system that allows the leader to disengage from the organization. Time-offs helps the leader to change focus, which is vital for physical, mental, and spiritual well-being.

A significant part of self-care is the management of personal relationships outside the scope of the assignment. The leaders need to look after themselves and what matters to them. The leaders should not lose themselves when helping others and fulfilling their assignments.

While they are not directly involved, friends and families of the leader are essential parts of the leadership assignment. Self-care involves caring for our relationships with people that are part of our lives. Every leadership assignment will end someday. The end of a leadership assignment does not signify the end of teams or organizations. When the team is no longer there, friends and families will be there. Every leader needs to nurture and grow personal relationships and build lives outside their assignments.

In my own life, I rank things around my life in this order: God, family and friends, and assignment. I will never give up my family and friends for my job. At the end of the assignment, I will return to them. I should remember them while I am still working on my assignment.

The leader is a human being that goes through issues of life like any other person. The internal and external well-being of the leader is crucial to the success of the organization. The leaders that care for themselves within and without are the one that can help their organizations and lead effectively. Leadership can be lonely, but self-care is universal.

CARING FOR ORGANIZATION

The core aspect of the assignment of any leader is to look after the well-being of the organization. In this context, the organization could be a family, work team, small business, charity organization, large corporation, religious organization, or country. The primary job of the leader is to protect the interests of the organization, ensure that the organization fulfills its mission, and delivers its promises to the customers. The leader must ensure that the organization is stable, healthy, and sustainable.

The leader cares by focusing on the growth, perception, productivity, effectiveness, efficiency, evolution, and adaptation of the organization. The leader also looks after the welfare of the team members, internal and external relationships, and customer expectations. Leadership care improves the chances of short-term and long-term organizational success.

The leader cares for the organization by ensuring that the organization is financially stable, operationally efficient, and compliant with all regulations. The organization must be stable internally while continuously improving, innovating, and agile. The leader builds a balanced and sustainable system and ensures that the organization is strategically positioned to compete.

Strategy, System, Process, And Procedure

Every organization is a system built on a web of interconnected processes. The system is a function of the organizational strategy as the internal setup depends on how the leaders intend to carry out the activities of the organization. The processes influence the effectiveness and efficiency of the system, and the procedure breaks down organizational activities.

Strategy is the formulated plan of action to achieve organizational goals. It clarifies how an organization approaches its businesses. The strategy determines how human resources, financial, operational, technological, marketing, and other business functions are combined to form the organizational system. On a lower level, each business function has strategies that are usually part of the broader organizational strategy. For example, a company that hires employees with high school diplomas has a different strategy from the company that hires employees with bachelor's degrees. The knowledge of the employees will affect the products and services of the company. The strategy also influences the organizational processes and individual business functional processes.

System is the structure or setup of an organization. The system defines reporting structure, communication flow, functional definition and roles, and how individuals fit into the organization. Every organization, regardless of the size or purpose, is a system. The organizational system comprises sub-systems such as management, operations, financial, human resources, compliance, technological, etc. The systems of larger corporations have more subsystems than smaller organizations. The system aligns teams, individuals, and processes to create an organizational environment.

Process is a series of interrelated or interacting actions or steps to achieve a goal. Processes occur at every level of the organization. There are organizational processes, functional business processes, and task processes. On an organizational level, hiring qualified employees for every job function is a process. On a functional level, the human resources processes include hiring, performance management, and benefits administration. On a task level, hiring an employee requires job advertisement, interviewing, and candidate selection processes.

Procedure is a step-by-step instruction or details on how to carry out a task. For example, the job advertisement above requires a procedure that includes when, what, how, who posts the job. The procedure will consist of details such as advertising medium, advertising duration, job posting content, application mode, etc. The procedure provides directions to meet the intended goal.

Process Efficiency And Effectiveness

A web of inter-connected processes sustains the organizational system. One or more processes connect the subsystems to ensure the smooth running of the organization. The efficiency of these processes determines the effectiveness of the sub-systems and the whole system. It is important to emphasize that everything that we do in life is a process. If the process is wrong, the outcome (product or service) will be faulty. The processes influence the relationships among the members, relationships with customers, and overall organizational activities.

The effectiveness of a process is the degree to which the series of actions produces the desired result. Process efficiency is the effort (time, energy, resources) required to achieve a business outcome. A process can be effective but not efficient and vice versa. The achievement of efficiency and effectiveness increases the quality of products and services while reducing waste and increasing profitability. Here are some of the ways to improve the efficiency and effectiveness of a process.

Process Mapping. A process map, also called workflow or flowchart, is a planning and management tool for identifying the series of tasks and responsible parties involved in a process. The purpose is to identify how business tasks are arranged to identify bottlenecks and redundancies within the system. A process map can help an organization reduce the time and cost of doing business while improving overall quality and return on investment. A process map can inform an organization of the need for business process re-engineering, business process improvement, or continuous improvement plans.

Business Process Re-engineering (BPR). This involves a fundamental rethinking of the entire organizational system, eliminating the current business process, and creating a new process. The goal of BPR is to achieve dramatic improvement in the areas of cost, quality, service, and speed of business. BPR has a broad scope as it affects every aspect of the organization. It also requires a lot of resources and commitment on the part of the organizational leaders.

Business Process Improvement (BPI). This is a gradual change in the business process. It has a smaller scope and focuses mainly on improving the quality and speed of certain parts of the organization. BPI can be a one-time project or ongoing program built into the system.

Continuous improvement. This is an ongoing improvement in the quality of products and services. Continuous improvement is built into the organizational system to continuously evaluate and improve the quality of products and services. It allows businesses to identify and fix problems quickly. Kaizen, which is one of the most popular continuous improvement programs in the world, prioritizes the process of achieving results above the results. Kaizen believes that imperfect processes will jeopardize the goal. Kaizen aims to streamline work, reduce waste, and improve the quality of the outcome. Other process improvement programs include Kaban, lean management, six sigma, and Total Quality Management.

Sustainable Organization

The long-term outlook of an organization is one of the primary goals of a good leader. The organization must continue when the current members are no longer part of the system. The makeup of the organization determines whether the organization will be sustainable without the leader. Good leaders create a system that is currently effective and sustainable for the future.

A sustainable organization has a sustainable system. The system is stable, dynamic, flexible, adaptable, and growing at the same time. The internal composition makes the organization responsive and ready for future challenges.

A sustainable system has easy entry and exit for people. Some organizational have individuals that are indispensable or irreplaceable. Those individuals are the only ones that know what to do. Please note that I am not encouraging organizations to see employees as disposables. The organization should be able to run smoothly when an employee, leader, or owner is no longer in the system. This process starts with the leader.

Unfortunately, some leaders have made themselves the system. They build the organization around themselves, and everything runs through them. Instead of building the organization, they build themselves. Some leaders do this due to a lack of trust. They minimize the influence of others and exert control over the system to always make themselves indispensable and relevant. Therefore, the leader cannot take his or her mind off the organization, rest, or take a vacation. The leader must always be at alert every time.

The leader needs to create a succession planning program so that the organization will continue with or without the leader. The leaders need to think about what happens when they are no longer part of the system. The leader needs to develop other leaders by providing growth opportunities.

Sustainable systems are built on effective processes and not individuals. There must be a clear process for every organizational activity. Everyone, including the leader, follows the process. The processes are supported by effective policies and procedures and not conscience.

Building organizations on conscience is not sustainable because human conscience is susceptible to corruption. Irrespective of how open and liberal any organization wants to be, policies and procedures are simply indispensable. Policies and procedures define the standards of behaviors and how to do things. Policies and procedures ensure consistency, equality, and fairness. Moreover, policies and procedures make it easy to deal with individuals with bad intentions. Good policies and procedures must not affect organizational agility and flexibility. The policies and procedures must accommodate innovation and creativity.

Every system starts and ends with the people. The leader must invest in the organizational members through training, mentoring, and personal development programs. Leaders need to aid the growth of their followers by providing them with challenges and opportunities. Leaders should develop their followers to become leaders. The more leaders in an organization, the more chances of success and sustainability.

Leadership does not necessarily have to do with titles or positions but psychological ability to take ownership of projects, jobs, and situations. The sustainability of a system depends on people. The higher the capability of the people, the higher the chances of productivity and efficiency. The contributions of the employees depend on their capacities. The leader must invest in building the capabilities of organizational members and help them to be successful.

Sustainable organizations are less complex or ambiguous. Complexity paralyzes the organizational system and restricts creativity that could position the organization for growth and development. Whenever it is difficult to make simple decisions because there are too many factors to be considered or too many layers, the organization is suffering from complexity. Complex organizations are usually stagnant and struggle to compete in the market. Complexity slows down decision-making and creativity. It also increases the cost of doing business. Complex organizations are unsustainable because they will not be agile enough to cope with environmental changes.

The leader also needs to remove uncertainty to create a sustainable organization. Life is full of uncertainties, but some uncertainties create chaos. For example, ambiguous processes, unclear expectations, lack of job securities, and vague strategies create uncertainties. Such uncertainties unsettle the system, reduce employee commitment, and promote gossip.

Some leaders keep everything closer to their chests. Everything within the organization is considered a top-secret, and no one can know what is going on. While every piece of information is not for everyone, organizational members should know enough to remain calm and remain focused. The leader must remove uncertainties from the system as much as possible. A cloud of uncertainty over an organization paralyzes the organizational activities. It creates panic and reduces the trust of employees and customers.

Internal Organizational Dynamics

Outside forces such as the economy, competitors, and regulation are threats to the existence of organizations. When the forces that divide an organization are greater than the forces that unite the organization, the organization will inevitably crumble. The internal dynamics of an organization determines whether the organization can withstand outside pressure.

I am a firm believer in the quote that "a house divided against itself cannot stand." An organization with a weak internal dynamic is susceptible to external threats and attacks because it has a weak immune system. It is easier for a competitor to target a divided organization than a united one. A united team fight for one another while a divided team fight one another.

Leaders are the architects of strong internal organizational dynamics. Unfortunately, some leaders are threatened by the unity of their followers because of the fear of mutiny. They sow discord among the followers and pitch them against one another. Such leaders employ divide and conquer techniques to control the system. The method could work for the short-term, but it is not a long-term management strategy. The technique usually ends up backfiring when the team members realize that the leader is dividing them. The followers can unite against the leader, and the fear of the leader will eventually come true.

One of the ways of creating a positive organizational dynamic is to crack down on negative behaviors. Behaviors such as yelling, backbiting, bullying, and other behaviors that could create a hostile working environment must be quickly dealt with and not given any room to thrive.

Negative behaviors create long-term problems by destroying peace and harmony. Some leaders think it takes too much to deal with drama, but the cost of negligence far exceeds the cost of dealing with the problem. The leader must ensure that negative behaviors are not allowed to thrive. Irrespective of the talent and skills, anyone with a toxic attitude should not be a part of the organization.

As a leader, it is essential to set behavioral standards that encourage respect. The culture of respect starts with the leader. The leader must respect his or her subordinates. When the leader leads by example by respecting everyone irrespective of the status or position, everyone will follow the lead and do the same.

I believe that it takes more to disrespect than to respect. Most times, we think that respecting others hurt our ego, but it actually enhances our ego. It is easy for people to relate to a respectful and humble individual than a rude and condescending person.

There is a common vice among leaders, and many do not know its effect on organizational dynamics. Many leaders have the habit of undercutting the other leaders that report to them. While some do this unknowingly, some intentionally weaken the influences of the leaders below them. Undercutting occurs when senior leaders address issues that junior leaders should address without consulting the junior leaders.

In the name of open communication, floor employees will bring issues to the middle or senior manager. Instead of the middle or senior manager to consult with the line manager, they will go ahead and solve the problem. While this looks like a proactive measure, the consequence is that floor employees will start to lose respect for the line managers and go above the line managers every time. Also, whenever the line manager brings up concerns, the floor employees will not listen. Open communication is excellent, but problems should be solved with the line manager and not without the line manager. Senior leaders should develop and empower other leaders that report to them.

Leaders need to avoid the creation of silos in organizations. Silos tend to develop when departments within the same organization view one another as competitors rather than collaborators. Individuals have loyalties towards one another within their teams but view the members of other departments as adversaries.

Some team leaders tend to create "we against them" in their followers to encourage their teams. This type of mentality creates silos within the organization and reduces collaboration that is essential for organizational success. Team leaders with silo mentalities need to understand that every department within the organization needs one another to succeed. Leaders must prevent silos from developing, and if it is already established, it must be dismantled.

One of the easiest ways for a leader to disrupt the internal organizational dynamics is favoritism towards an employee, team, or department. Favoritism diminishes the trust of followers in the leader because the other employees will feel that there is nothing they could do to get noticed. They will also think that the favored employee or team is untouchable. Favoritism could lead to loss of commitment, lack of trust, and turnover.

Sometimes in life, it is difficult not to have someone that we prefer among many people. However, leaders need to avoid making it obvious. Favoritism does not only affect others, but it also hurts the favored. The achievements or talents of the favored will always be minimized and be attributed to favoritism.

The leaders who understand the importance of positive team dynamics to the success of their organizations do everything possible to promote unity, peace, harmony, and teamwork among the members. The leaders encourage the team member to respect and help one another. They do not encourage artificial harmony or unnecessary competition. It is worth noting that not all competitions are bad, but competition must not overtake the purpose of the task or team.

Internal organizational dynamics influence knowledge sharing, organizational commitment, organizational citizenship behaviors, employee turnover, teamwork, and collaboration. In an organization or team with a positive internal dynamic, there will be interpersonal relationships and trust, which are essential for teamwork and knowledge sharing. The followers see themselves as part of the bigger group, and everyone will work towards the common goal. It also enhances creativity as team members will find it easier to share ideas without fear of anyone taking credit for their ideas.

Trust among members and the trust of the leader is

essential for a positive organizational dynamic. Trust is the bedrock of teamwork and interpersonal relationships. The followers must be able to work together and with the leader with open minds and without reservations. The followers must not doubt the intentions of the leader. The leader must create a control system for checks and balances, but the leader must trust the followers to do their jobs and not micromanage them.

A positive dynamic is a force that can make teams successful. Positivity does not indicate an absence of conflict or disagreement. Positive dynamics encourage disagreement because team members know that they can overcome their disagreement and come to a positive conclusion. Disagreement is not always the problem; how the team handles the disagreement is usually the problem. The organizational environment must be conducive for people to express themselves and respectfully disagree. Positive team dynamics enhance trust and cooperation, which is needed to gain a competitive advantage in the marketplace.

External Organizational Perception

The leadership care for the organization must not neglect the outside perception of the organization. The relationship between the organization and its environment is crucial to the success of the organization. The external perception creates a reputation for the organization, which affects how people relate to the organization. The perception also affects how the organization attracts employees, customers, and partners.

The factors that affect the reputation of an organization include its mission, values, contribution and commitment to the environment and community, quality of product and services, customer relationships, employee and vendor treatment, among others. The leader must bear in mind that the current and future success of the organization depends on how people perceive the organization. The perception gives people the impression of the organization and determines whether people will trust whatever comes from the organization. The organization must be dependable and trustworthy.

The reputation of the organization affects the image of individuals within the organization, especially the leaders. Employees want to trust their employers, partners want to trust their allies, citizens want to trust their leaders, kids want to trust their parents, and church members want to trust their pastors. When leaders care for the image of the organization, the leaders care for their image.

Caring For Organization

Leadership care for the organization affects the success of the organization. Caring leaders put their egos and interests aside to further the interest of their organizations. They focus on building dynamic and sustainable organizations.

Leadership care for the organization starts from within. The external image of the organization is mostly a reflection of the internal image. A poorly managed organization will have a poor image. An organization can have a nice logo and website, and the vision, mission, and values could have compelling words. Yet, the external image must reflect the inner beauty. Leaders must learn to build from within. Some leaders focus on cosmetics than the reputation of the organization. The cosmetics must be in addition to the right strategies, efficient and effective processes, positive internal dynamics, solid financial standings, sound policies and procedures, and quality products and services.

Good leaders think about the future of the organization every time. They plan for the current events with one eye on the future. We have seen leaders that trade the future of their organizations for short-term gains. They do not care about what happens after they leave the organization. They leave a terrible system that will make things difficult for their successors. Their goal is to make their successors look bad so that people can appreciate them more.

Good leaders do not only think about themselves and their assignments. They care about the success of their subordinates and successors. They create systems that bring the best out of everyone and prepare the organization for the future. They build the organization to compete now and in the future.

The leaders who care about their organizations have a succession plan to ensure continuity even after they are no longer in the system. According to a friend and a mentor, Kathy Kasten, succession planning should start the same day that the assignment begins. Good leaders know that they will not be in the organization forever. They plan, develop people, and create systems with the transition in mind. They consider the success of their successors an extension of their accomplishments.

CARING FOR RESULT

For every assignment, there will always be an expectation of results. Irrespective of the size or nature of the assignment, every leader will be judged by the results. The leader will be judged in terms of profit, return on investments, problems solved, lives touched, and influenced. The leader will also be judged based on the productivity, effectiveness, and efficiency of their systems. The outcome of every effort and passion will be evident by the result.

The result of the leadership efforts has implications for leaders. It could affect the career and future job prospects of the leader. For business owners, the results could affect the current and future business endeavors. In governments, the result could affect the electability of the leader and future political aspirations. The outcome of the leadership assignment is significant. For example, the board of directors of companies will look for a business leader with good results. Politicians with track records of success can point to their accomplishments when campaigning for offices.

Definition Of Result

The definition of the expected result is an essential step in the assessment of any assignment. Result is the outcome or product of action, but the actual definition of result varies based on the task at hand. It is unwise to embark on a journey without a clear idea of the destination or an adequate understanding of the expectations.

The first thing that a leader needs to do is to identify who is expecting the results. The people expecting results include business owners, citizens of a country, congregation, boards of directors, family members, and many others. Some business owners who are also leaders sometimes have a false sense of security. They believe that they owe no one an explanation. While this is true in some sense, it is ultimately false. Business owners are accountable to families and friends, customers, and the part of themselves that expects results. If the business is not successful, the business owner has failed him or herself. Sometimes, friends and families will pay the price for their failures.

After identifying those expecting results, the leader needs to clarify expectations and be realistic. Some leaders take on assignments without clarifying expectations. They embark on an endless journey. Lack of understanding of the expectation will not allow the leader to answer crucial questions along the way. Are there enough resources to get the desired result? Do we have enough time to achieve our goals? Are we on the right track?

The result of every leadership assignment could either be a success or a failure. There is not much of a middle ground between success and failure. We sometimes politely say that the outcome is mixed, but this is ultimately a failure. To make it plain, you are either succeed or fail as a leader. Leaders must know what success and failure look like for their assignments. The apparent and straightforward metric of success in a for-profit business is profit. Peace and economic prosperity are the metrics of success for a political regime. Successful and well-behaved children are the metrics of success of good parenting. However, the actual metric can be different based on the details of the assignment. Some leaders are recruited to stabilize a chaotic organization, while some are recruited to make the organization profitable.

While the result of a leadership assignment could be described in a short sentence, the leader needs to break down the big result into smaller outcomes based on small goals with timelines. As stated above, goals must build on one another. The leadership assignment can be likened to a student whose goal is to receive a degree or diploma. The student will attend several classes with different homework and exams. For each of the classes, the student needs to know the rubric and what it takes to succeed.

When defining the result of a leadership assignment, the leader must analyze the current state of the system, identify success requirements, the time frame for achieving the results, and how success will be measured. The knowledge will help the leader assemble the right team, develop a plan, and determine the required resources. For example, a leader who takes over a struggling business might have high employee turnover, bad public image, low-quality product, poor financial performance, poor customer relationship, and many others. The leader faces an enormous task, but the leader needs to clarify expectations and how the board of directors will define success. If the expected result is to make the organization profitable, the leader must solve all the problems listed above and many more.

Uber changed the way we imagine the transportation system, but the organization is in chaos. Uber is not profitable and has a negative public image, among other issues. The company hired Dara Khosrowshahi to lead the organization in the right direction. Before the new CEO can make Uber profitable, he must stabilize the internal organization, improve employee morale by creating a new organizational culture, and repair Uber's public image. Facing a problem like that of Uber, the new CEO must define the expectations before embarking on the assignment.

Sometimes, the expectations of an assignment might change based on the analysis and the prevailing conditions. The assignment of Marissa Meyer as the CEO of Yahoo comes to mind. Her task was to make Yahoo relevant again so that the company can compete with Google and Facebook. However, reality suggested that Yahoo will not compete with the two giants despite several unsuccessful efforts and investments. From the market perspective, her result was considered mixed. Some thought that her tenure as an outright failure because she did not achieve the desired outcome. However, she got a fairly good return for the investors after the sale of Yahoo.

Leaders can analyze assignments and identify success criteria based on the outcomes of the past successful and failed leaders. The study of the results of the other leaders can help leaders to shape their assignments and define success. The leader can also draw on personal experiences of failure and success when approaching future tasks. Leaders like Dara and Marissa will draw from their experiences as they approach the next chapters of their careers. Previous experiences and lessons learned from others help leaders work toward the desired result. After clarifying the expected result, the leader must build for the desired result.

Building For Results

Success in leadership does not come overnight; it requires adequate preparation. Great leaders build their teams for success so that success can become part of the team's DNA. The leader needs to assemble the right team and secure the resources. The scale of the assignment determines the size of the resources and skillsets of the teams. For example, a multinational company leader will consider the impact of technology, language, culture, political landscape, among other factors. These considerations will help the leader assemble the team with the right skillsets to handle the tasks and allocate resources to deliver results.

One of the primary reasons leaders fail to achieve the desired result is their inability to assemble the right team. The leader cannot do everything based on personal strengths or wisdom. As they say, it takes a village to raise a child; it takes a team to deliver results. The success of every leader depends on their team. Once the leader realizes this, it will help them to assemble the right team. Some leaders overestimate their strengths or do not want to share the glory with their teams. Leaders must realize that they are as good as their teams because they are responsible for the success or failure of their teams. A bad team is a reflection of a bad leader because the leader builds the team.

The quality of results depends on the quality of the team. A team is a group of individuals that come together to achieve a common goal. While teamwork is critical, we cannot neglect the impact of individual personality and capabilities. When building results, leaders need to work on the composition of their teams. A good team has knowledgeable and competent individuals in various roles. Apart from individual competencies, all team members must have the right personality to work as part of a unified team. Every capable individual will not be a good team member because some individuals are more focused on personal glory than the success of the team. Such individuals can divide the team and create a toxic environment. The leader must ensure that the team has the right balance of competence and personality.

The purpose of the team is to compensate for the weaknesses of the leader. To have a balanced team, the leader must be open to different ideas and personalities and not recruit people that think the same way. Diversity is the strength of every team. When we talk about diversity, most people automatically assume it is about race or gender. Although race and gender are crucial, there is more to diversity. Diversity includes perspectives, competencies, experience, ideas, personalities, knowledge, and strengths. Diversity prevents continuous group thinking because of the variety of ideas. While everyone is working towards the same goal, there is a strong need for different perspectives. Some people even say that every team needs at least a "devil's advocate." Devil's advocates are individuals that will criticize or question your intentions or make you second guess your thoughts and ideas. These people help teams to review their products or ideas to identify potential issues. Pessimists can help teams anticipate problems so that the team can prepare for them.

Some leaders do not like to be challenged or made to rethink their ideas or decisions. To prevent that, they silence everyone who opposes their ideas, stop listening, or purposefully assemble a team of "yes men and women." The leaders that are building for results are not afraid of being criticized or challenged. Such leaders revel in criticisms because it helps them to see their flaws and work harder.

After assembling a good team, the leader must communicate the vision and break it down into smaller goals. The leader will set the team on the path for success by setting and clarifying expectations, delegating responsibilities, set acceptable standards, and create an accountability system. The leader needs to let everyone know how they contribute to the success of the team and continually communicate the expected result.

The leaders that are building for results can be overbearing and demanding at times, but good leaders know how to bring their teams together so that everyone can see the bigger picture. Being a demanding leader is not necessarily a problem, but the problem lies in the approach and purpose. The questions to be asked include: Is demand for the greater good or the leader only? Is there a balanced approach to the demands? Do others also learn good work ethics and become better individuals? There are times when the team needs to do more than enough to get the desired result. Leaders must recognize the sacrifices of their team and find ways to compensate them in the long run.

The leader must set ground rules in the team from the beginning. Failure to lay down the ground rules at the beginning will cause the leader to be playing catchup, which complicates the assignment. Every team member must know what is acceptable and what is not acceptable right from the start. The team must know the "non-negotiables" such as quality of work, hard work, honesty, transparency, respect, and teamwork. Ground rules help the team to stay focused and hold everyone accountable, including the leader. It helps the leader to identify and weed out bad eggs. It also helps the leader to be fair and consistent.

The Result Orientation

In sports, we usually hear about the heart of a champion. Talents are never enough, but the team with a winning mentality always wins. Such teams show up at the right time and put up the performance needed to succeed. They know what it means to win and how to win even when their backs are against the wall. This mentality is applicable in every aspect of life. It is vital to have a talented team. However, the difference between winners and losers lies mostly in their mentalities.

Mental strengths become apparent when things are not going in the right direction or there is a significant challenge. Everyone can lead when the going is good, but a good leader emerges when things get complicated, and the team is struggling. The key to achieving results when things are not going well lies in the mental composition of the team.

Good leaders deliver results by team spirit and human management. One-time motivation is not enough to deliver results; it is a process. Good leaders build result orientation into their teams and prepare their team for difficult moments. They develop excellent team spirit and prepare their teams to get results. They allow their teams to view team results as individual results. The team orientation kicks on when the going gets tough.

As the team continues to grow, the leader does not need to emphasize the results often. At a point, the team would have developed a natural appetite for success. The desire for success becomes part of the DNA. Everyone understands what it takes to get results and know that failure is not an option even under challenging circumstances. When there is a setback, the team knows how to bounce back.

Good leaders achieve results without breaking the

law or taking advantage of others. They are careful not to become successful at the expense of their teams, customers, or the future of the organization. Some people equate winning mentality to law-breaking, bullying, and taking advantage of people. True winning is not breaking the law; it is being victorious despite the law. Great leaders dig deeper, use their resources, tap into the depth of their team, motivate the team, emotionally connect with their team, and explore the creativity of their teams.

In team sports, great coaches that win over a long period build their teams for long-term success. In the search for immediate results, some coaches sacrifice the future of their teams. The wall will start crumbling after one or two years. Sometimes, wise leaders sacrifice short term success for long term success because they see beyond what everyone sees. They build their team to get to the desired destination by small incremental successes rather than getting a one-time unsustainable success. Some leaders could still deliver significant results in the short term, but they never lose sight of long-term success.

Sustaining The Result

The strength to build for results is different from the strength to sustain the results. Individual personalities affect their ability to build and sustain results. Some leaders are builders, some are sustainers, and some are hybrids of builders and sustainers.

Builders are pure entrepreneurs. They are very enterprising and find it easy to get results but sometimes struggle to sustain the momentum. They are risk-takers and can build an edifice out of nothing. Builders can spot talents, influence people, and inspire them to do the unthinkable.

However, most builders can become victims of their successes. Ego can sometimes set in, and their accomplishments get into their heads. They are very intense and can be bored easily because they love to keep building. Their personalities can make it difficult for them to sustain the result.

Sustainers can also build, but it is not their core strength. They are skilled in sustaining results over time. They are not big risk-takers because they might lack the personality to be intensive and push things through every time. Sustainers have grace, humility, and patience to work with people. It is easy for them to keep their egos in check. They do not mind sharing the glory as long as the team benefits.

There are rare hybrids of builders and sustainers who know which card to use at every point. They know when to be intense or pull back. They know when to be patient and go for it. Hybrid leaders find it easy to attract and retain people. They know how to cater to people of different personalities.

Builders and sustainers can develop themselves to gain new skills. However, it is difficult for people to be who they are not. One way to get the best of both worlds is to partner with people with different strengths. Builders and sustainers have unique abilities and need each other. If they can work together and respect each other's strengths, they can become an unstoppable force.

The leader can sustain the result through continuous engagement with the team. The leader ensures that the team is engaged and does not lose sight of the goal. The leader ensures that followers take pride in their work and accomplishments. The leader gives the followers credit for success and lets them enjoy the benefits of success.

The leader must be careful and not take success or competence for granted. The leader must continue to provide resources and oversight for the team. The *Nuts Island Effect* by Paul F. Levy depicts an organization that became a victim of its success. In the article, the leaders became distracted by political engagements. They disengaged from a talented and dedicated team that will solve problems to keep the operations going. The leaders assumed that the team was self-sufficient, and the autonomy of the followers was taken for granted. As the team grew stronger, they resented the leaders. The team started marking their own rules, which eventually led to a disaster. The leaders set the team up for success but could not sustain success because they lost focus and took success for granted.

The hard work of building a success mentality will go to waste if not sustained. It is deceptive to assume that the team will continue to work with the success mindset without encouragement. The leader needs to continue to encourage and challenge the team to sustain the mentality. It is easy for successful teams to become complacent and rest on their laurels.

The feeling of invincibility of high-flying teams can lead to complacency. The team can become arrogant and self-destruct. The leader needs to keep the team humble, set new and higher expectations, break new grounds, and challenge the team. It is good to celebrate successes, but the team must stay grounded and be ready for the next challenge. The leader needs to encourage new ideas so that everyone is excited and challenged.

The leader also needs to ensure that the team continues to improve in every aspect. The leader needs to encourage individual and overall improvement. The team must know that there is always room for improvement.

The team cannot take its eye off the goal or feel that it has achieved everything. We live in a dynamic world, and the team must be actively engaged. The leader must ensure that the organization is agile and flexible enough to adopt new ideas and improve.

Leading organizations such as Kodak and many media giants struggled or went out of business at the beginning of the 21st century because they stopped improving. When the internet of things began, those industry giants were left behind. The problem lies at the doors of leaders that failed to sustain their long-term success. The organizations did not evolve to keep up with the changes.

Caring For Results

Leaders are not just figureheads; they are in leadership roles for specific purposes. Their purpose is to produce results to justify the need for their roles. The leaders that understand their assignments know that there are expectations of results. They care for every aspect of the organization while keeping their eyes on the goal.

Caring for results is not negotiable for leaders. Every leader that did not produce results will be considered a failure. While the result is the product of all the efforts, it is the focal point of the assignment. All other leadership caring must produce results. The leader must build the structure and system with people, processes, and resources to get the result.

The demand for results is continuous. The achievement of one goal raises expectations and increases demands. Leaders cannot rest on the laurels and allow their teams to become complacent. For every individual in the organization, the expectation is to produce results. The need for results in a leadership role is more critical because the survival of the organization depends on the leadership results.

CARING FOR PEOPLE

Businesses are done by the people, with the people, and for the people. Whenever we are talking about an organization, we are talking about the people that make up the organization. Irrespective of the purpose of an organization, people are the reasons for its existence. We have people in various capacities, such as owners, leaders, employees, citizens, volunteers, customers, teachers, and players.

The purpose of organizations, teams, nations, or any establishment is towards people. Countries are in existence because of citizens, sports teams are for fans and supporters, schools are for students, religious organizations are for members, and business products and services are for people, including business to business companies.

Every leadership vision and assignment that does not care for people is propaganda for a self-serving purpose. Organizational products and services are developed by people and aimed at people. Even when we use computer programs and robots to build products, human beings create and control robots, and the outcomes are for human use or consumption.

Every leadership decision must have a strong consideration for human outcomes. We have seen many leadership decisions that impact the followers negatively. Many times, the leaders suffer little to no consequences for their poor choices. While some leaders could lose their jobs or companies, many of them have generous severance packages. In addition to that, many of them can easily restart their lives because of their networks and privileges. Some leaders make poor financial decisions, lead ineffective organizations, have poor product lines, and create a poor working environment. The vulnerable people are left to deal with the consequences of the decisions that they did not make. Some people never recover from job losses due to certain factors such as age and stage of life.

The actions and inactions of the leaders during the financial crisis are typical examples of poor leadership decisions that affected several innocent people worldwide. The governments failed to regulate poor lending practices while leaders of financial institutions made risky investments. While few business leaders were prosecuted, and some companies were penalized, several vulnerable people were at the losing end of the poor decisions. The big companies were deemed too big to fail and got bailed out, but many small businesses lost everything. As a result of the poor choices, many people around the world lost their jobs, homes, cars, retirement benefits, and many more. Some people could not retire as planned, while some people committed suicide because they thought everything was over.

Human beings are the reasons why organizations or institutions exist. It is impossible to eliminate the impact of people on organizations or institutions and vice versa. Leaders must think about those at the receiving end of their decisions and what becomes of the people.

Business And Humanity

One of the most popular phrases in the corporate world is: "This is business." People usually use the phrase to justify specific actions or behaviors, especially inhumane ones. Every business decision affects people because business is all about people. At the same time, businesses do not change who we are as human beings. During business transactions, our actions are more of a reflection of who we are rather than the business transactions.

It is worth noting that business decisions and humanity are not mutually exclusive; they complement each other. Considering human beings in business does not mean leaders will not make difficult decisions that will affect people. Consideration for people means that leaders will consider the impacts of their decisions on people and find the best way to mitigate the adverse effects. Leaders must make decisions with the least negative impacts on people. For example, leaders will not lay people off, reduce the quality of products, introduce products and services that could harm people when there are alternatives with less harm to people.

It is difficult to make decisions when an organization is in crisis. Leaders are responsible for making decisions, but their decisions should not be at the expense of the people they are supposed to serve. Leadership is a call to service, and decisions that do not consider people do not fulfill the requirements of the call.

Means To An End Or An End

Immanuel Kant, one of the most famous philosophers of the 18th century, challenged us to treat people, including ourselves, in a certain way. He said, "act in such a way that you treat humanity, whether in your own person or in the person of any other, never merely as a means to an end, but always at the same time as an end." There have been many debates about what Kant was talking about, but I take it exactly how I see it.

A means to an end means using people as tools to achieve a goal or a bridge to a destination. It does not mean that we will not do things through others or need their help. It means we should not view or use anyone or even ourselves as a tool to achieve a goal. We should not be willing to further our causes, maximize benefits, or build a reputation while damaging others.

Unfortunately, some leaders see the people under their influence as a means to an end. They see people as tools that can be used and discarded at any time. Some leaders can quickly identify the strengths and weaknesses of their followers and use the information to their advantage. Some leaders see influential followers that can galvanize people as tools to sell bad ideas to people. Instead of nurturing the strength, they ride on the reputation of the follower to carry out immoral agendas.

Some leaders exploit the weaknesses of their followers. Some individuals cannot say "No" or disagree with people. Once some leaders identify this weakness, they exploit it by using the follower to carry out immoral acts. Some employees want to please their bosses. Some leaders use it as an opportunity to make the employee carry out illegal and immoral acts. Some individuals need affirmation and reassurance that they will do everything possible to get the praise of the leader. Some leaders view such individuals as tools of oppression. Some followers are also morally bankrupt; such are essential tools for immoral leaders.

One of the flaws of charismatic leadership is the ability of the leaders to manipulate their followers. Charismatic leaders can lie to their followers and exploit them as much as possible. They can tell people what they want to hear when they know that the ideas are impractical. The leader can manipulate followers by convincing them that he or she is doing the right thing while carrying out self-serving agendas.

Some leaders view their citizens, customers, members, and employees as a means to an end. They have harmful products and programs that enrich them but harm their followers. The outcome of the people rarely factors into their thoughts.

Every leader needs to ask him or herself: Am I a User or a Developer? A user leader sees people as a means to an end. For users, every relationship is parasitic. They focus solely on what they can get. What they can give rarely crosses their minds. They cannot make sacrifices for others or share the benefits of a relationship. Anything that adds value to others does not interest them.

A developer leader sees people as an end. For developers, the mutual benefits of relationships are important to them. They focus on what they can do for others than what they can get. They provide opportunities for their followers to gain new skills while the followers contribute to the organization.

Good leaders think about the growth and development of their followers in everything that they do. They do not elevate their success above that of their followers. They contribute to the growth of their followers by creating programs that add value to their followers. They see the development of their followers as a personal benefit. They derive their satisfaction from the achievements of their followers.

Total Care For People

The leader must care for the followers as whole beings. Individual needs might differ due to several factors. The leaders might not meet every need, but they must be willing to go the extra length to help. Leaders that care for their people will explore available means to meet the needs of their people.

The leader must care about the physical well-being of the followers. As the famous saying goes, health is wealth. The health of the followers must be of utmost importance to the leader. The leader must make provisions for their followers to be healthy. The work environment must support the physical well-being of the employees. In companies, the chairs and table must support their well-being. The environment must be free of hazards, and the risk of injuries must be minimal. Healthy employees are more productive and psychologically focused.

The leader must care for the emotional and psychological well-being of the followers. Organizational factors such as process and procedures, clarity of purpose, work hours, flexibility, teamwork, honesty, trust, and interpersonal relationships among the followers impact the emotional and psychological well-being of the people. These factors minimize uncertainties, anxiety, and disagreements within the organization. For example, poor processes and conflicting information cause disagreements among people. The leaders must ensure that expectations are clarified and information flow consistently and without distortion within the organization.

The leader must care for the personal development and career growth of the followers. The leader can help aid the growth and development of the followers by assisting followers in identifying their talents and strengths. Studies have shown that focus on the strengths of the followers has positive impacts on job satisfaction or longevity. Focus on the strengths of the followers help the follower to grow personally and professionally. When individuals work in their areas of strength, they produce better results that add value to the organization and increase job satisfaction. The leader must be intentional and purposefully help the followers to grow. Caring for the growth and development of the followers benefit both the followers and the organization.

Investment of time, energy, and resources in people is an integral part of caring for people. The leader should provide followers with the opportunities to face challenges that will help them grow and develop their potential. The leadership investment in people is not only morally right, but it also has a significant return on investment.

Some leaders are afraid of investing in their followers because they believe that their followers will leave the company when the followers gain the necessary skills. People can leave the organization after investment. However, a leader that only invests people for immediate gain lacks foresight. Some leaders stop investing in their followers because of their experiences. The leadership investment in people is a long-term investment and not immediate, and the leader should know that all investments will not yield the desired result. Some followers will never repay the investment because of several factors such as the time, place, and individual personality.

Some investments will only yield results after the employees leave the organization. I have seen a situation whereby a leader developed the follower only for the follower to leave for a bigger organization after gaining the necessary skills. After a few years, the follower recommended the leader for contracts in the bigger organization.

Leadership care must go beyond the immediate work environment. Total leadership care for followers includes the immediate family members of the followers. Individual family situations affect productivity and output. The knowledge of the family situations of the followers helps the leader to care for the followers accordingly. If possible, it is good for the leaders to know the family situation and family members of the followers. The information can help the leader to help the followers. The leader can ensure that the followers feel safe and comfortable to talk about their families.

Emotional intelligence is an essential leadership skill. The leader must pay attention to the facial expressions of the followers and be able to understand their emotional state. Knowledge of the emotional state of individuals is a significant part of caring. Most times, a simple "how are you?" can make a difference. Sometimes, listening can help followers to navigate their problems. Some followers need a shoulder to lean on in times of crisis. A caring leader can be the shoulder in turbulent times.

A significant part of leadership caring is feedback. The leader should appreciate the followers for their efforts. The leader should be sensitive enough not to take credit for the work of the followers. The recognition of efforts could help or destroy the self-esteem and morale of some individuals.

Leadership caring shapes the perspective of the followers about the leader and the organization. Followers with leaders that care tend to be loyal to the leaders. Sometimes ago, I asked an employee why she is so loyal to her boss. She said,

My boss takes total care of me. He does not care for

me because of the job. He cares for me because he sees me as a person. He cares about my career, health, and family. My boss is the first person I talk to when things are not going well. If I want to make a career choice, get a degree, or make changes, my boss is always there. I am loyal to my boss because he is not helping me so that I can continue to work for him or because of his interest. My boss wants me to grow personally and professionally. He helps me through difficult moments, and I feel that I owe my successes to him. My boss told me that he is preparing me to be independent of him.

Caring is reciprocal. When the leader cares for people, people will care for the leader. As part of my discussion with the employee, she said she can never hide anything from my boss or do anything to hurt him because he cares. She feels obliged to take care of her boss and his business. She told me that she babysits his kids whenever his boss and his wife need to go out. She said she works so hard because she knows that he will take care of every other thing. She believes that she does not have anything to worry about because he cares.

As humans, we usually feel obliged to reciprocate the good deeds of others towards us. Organizational tasks are essential. However, focusing on tasks and neglecting people who will take care of the tasks is futile. When leaders take care of people, people will take care of the job. Leaders can use one stone to kill two birds by taking care of people because taking care of people is indirectly taking care of the work. Vision, assignment, money, results, knowledge, and power revolves around people. When we take care of people, people will take care of all these things. Without people, there is no leader. It is logically, morally, and intellectually essential to take care of people.

Some leaders value the bottom line more than people. The leader must care for the result, but the leader can achieve the result through caring for people. When leaders take care of the followers and always there in times of need, the followers will take care of all other things. Leaders need people to get the desired result.

Caring For People

Every leader must realize that leadership means having people under your charge. Simon Sinek said, "Leadership is not about being in charge; it is about taking care of people in your charge." The success of every leadership assignment depends on the people. If you are not taking care of the people in your charge, you have failed in your assignment. People make leaders because people are the reason why anyone can be a leader. People are the reason why that family, nation, company, business, church, nonprofit exist. Leadership caring is a two-way street. When the leader cares for the people, people will care for the leader.

It is important to emphasize that accountability and demand for better performance are not inhumane. The leader that does not hold followers accountable does not care for the assignment or people. The failure of the assignment could affect followers negatively as they could lose their jobs and income. Moreover, followers that are not accountable will not improve and grow.

Leaders must create a balance between care and productivity. I have seen some leaders who would avoid holding followers accountable so that the followers will not be angry, offended, or leave the organization. Such a view about leadership care is counterproductive. Leaders should not be afraid to hold their followers to a higher standard and have crucial conversations when needed.

Leadership care is not against truth as long as it is for encouragement and not spite. Some leaders prevent their followers from knowing critical truth to protect their followers. Preventing followers from knowing the truth does not help anyone.

Leadership starts and ends with the leader, but it is not about the leader. The earlier every leader understands this, the better the chances of success. Leadership is simply about the people that are under the charge of the leader. The behaviors and perspective of the leader influence the outcome, but the outcome affects people. In every leadership assignment, people must always be at the center. The role of the leader is to care, and people will make the assignment a success.

The people follow the leader and depend on the leader for direction, hope, and care. A good leader must guide people and prioritize their well-being. The leader creates a vision and sets the tone, but the people carry out the assignment.

FINAL WORDS

The missing piece in many assignments is leadership care. Every good and bad thing starts at the top, and so is caring. When leaders care, others will care. The leader needs to have the right attitude and passion, and people will do the remaining. Many nations, businesses, and organizations would have been more successful, but their leaders do not care enough to lead people to the promised land. Whatever matters to the leader matters to people. As long as people find purpose and direction, people will do their best to achieve their goals.

Caring is the basic requirement for every leader, yet the world is full of many leaders that do not care. Many of them are busy with activities, but they are passionate about the wrong things. Every leader must start caring about their assignments and the people under their care.

Leadership caring begins with the simple step of taking time to understand the assignment and its requirements. Questions such as the following and more will help the leader to start caring:

What is my assignment, and how can I be successful?

What are the expectations, and who is expecting results?

Why am I leading this team?

Am I in the right frame of mind to lead this team?

Who are my people, and am I adding value to them?

Am I managing money and other resources properly?

Caring does not mean carrying all the burden and being busy. It means putting an effective system in place with efficient processes that maximize the skills of people and resources with oversight for human and organizational benefits. Caring requires full involvement and engagement. The leader can be active, but it does not mean that the leader cares. Caring for everything does not mean that the leader must do everything. Leadership caring also involves knowing personal limitations and allowing professionals to do their jobs.

Caring helps leaders take a more in-depth look into their assignments. It helps the leader to be more connected and creative. Caring is not a one-time emotional sensation; it is a constant affection for the assignment and the people involved. Irrespective of our jobs or position, everyone can get better at caring when we are open, flexible, and adaptable. We all need to stop worrying and start caring. Worrying destroys assignments and people, but caring creates a path to success and build people.

This book starts with the assignment and ends with

people. I have never seen a successful establishment with a careless leader. The success of every leader is a function of the assignment and people. Vision guides the assignment and creates a beautiful destination, but the people will take the assignment to that destination. As long as the leader cares, success is guaranteed.

SPECIAL THANKS

Tekedia Institute
www.tekedia.com

Loving Touch Productions
www.lovingtouchproductions.com

Lion Crest Leadership
www.lioncrestleadership.com

Connaissance Impact
www.connaissanceimpact.com

www.ingramcontent.com/pod-product-compliance
Lightning Source LLC
Chambersburg PA
CBHW020440220526
45464CB00002B/785